VISUAL™
Quick Tips
Golf

Visual®

by Cheryl Anderson, Brian A. Crowell,
and Tom Mackin

Wiley Publishing, Inc.

Praise for the VISUAL Series

I just had to let you and your company know how great I think your books are. I just purchased my third Visual book (my first two are dog-eared now!) and, once again, your product has surpassed my expectations. The expertise, thought, and effort that go into each book are obvious, and I sincerely appreciate your efforts. Keep up the wonderful work!

—Tracey Moore (Memphis, TN)

I have several books from the Visual series and have always found them to be valuable resources.

—Stephen P. Miller (Ballston Spa, NY)

Thank you for the wonderful books you produce. It wasn't until I was an adult that I discovered how I learn—visually. Although a few publishers out there claim to present the material visually, nothing compares to Visual books. I love the simple layout. Everything is easy to follow. And I understand the material! You really know the way I think and learn. Thanks so much!

—Stacey Han (Avondale, AZ)

Like a lot of other people, I understand things best when I see them visually. Your books really make learning easy and life more fun.

—John T. Frey (Cadillac, MI)

I am an avid fan of your Visual books. If I need to learn anything, I just buy one of your books and learn the topic in no time. Wonders! I have even trained my friends to give me Visual books as gifts.

—Illona Bergstrom (Aventura, FL)

I write to extend my thanks and appreciation for your books. They are clear, easy to follow, and straight to the point. Keep up the good work! I bought several of your books and they are just right! No regrets! I will always buy your books because they are the best.

—Seward Kollie (Dakar, Senegal)

Credits

Acquisitions Editor
Pam Mourouzis

Copy Editor
Carol Pogoni

Editorial Manager
Christina Stambaugh

Publisher
Cindy Kitchel

Vice President and Executive Publisher
Kathy Nebenhaus

Interior Design
Kathie Rickard
Elizabeth Brooks

Cover Design
José Almaguer

Photography
Fred Vuich

Additional Photography
Tom Mackin
(pages 22, 25 (top), 80, 81, 152 (top),
158, 161, 162, 164 (bottom), 165,
167 (top), 169)

Photographic Assistant
Michael Cohen

About the Authors

Cheryl Anderson teaches at the Mike Bender Golf Academy in Lake Mary, Florida. She received the 2006 National Teacher of the Year award and the 2007 Metropolitan PGA Teacher of the Year award. She is one of *Golf for Women* magazine's 50 Top Women Teachers in America. Cheryl also is one of the best woman club pro competitors ever. In 2004 she earned the Metropolitan PGA Section Women's Player of the Year award for a record fifth consecutive season. She also was runner-up in the 2002 LPGA National Club Professional Championship and has competed in numerous LPGA Tour events. A graduate of Rutgers University, Cheryl is a Class A member of both the LPGA and the PGA of America. She has  authored numerous instruction articles for *Golf for Women, The Met Golfer,* and *Golf Digest Woman.*

Brian Crowell has been helping his students enjoy the game of golf since 1991. He has held the position of Head Golf Professional since 1997 and is currently employed at GlenArbor Golf Club in Bedford, New York.

In addition to his volunteer work for various charities and programs, Brian has served on the Education Committee of the Metropolitan PGA since 1996 and was the Chairman from 2002 through 2005. In 2003, he was awarded the prestigious Horton Smith Award for his outstanding contributions to education. In 2005, he was elected to the Executive Committee and currently serves as a board member of the Metropolitan Section.

Brian is a highly regarded instructor in the Metropolitan Section and beyond. He has given countless individual lessons and clinics and has authored numerous instructional articles. His work has been featured in Donald Trump's book *The Best Golf Advice I Ever Received* and in *The Secret of Golf* by George Peper. He has also contributed to many newspapers and magazines, including recent issues of *GOLF Magazine.* In 2003, National Consumers Research named Brian one of America's Best Instructors, and he is very proud to have been selected as a Top 50 Kids Teacher for 2005 by U.S. Kids Golf.

Brian has been seen in national television commercials with Craig Stadler. He is the creator, host, and producer of *The Clubhouse*, a golf radio show that can be heard Wednesdays from 7 to 8 pm on AM1230 WFAS. He is also a frequent instruction contributor for AM1050 ESPN. As a broadcast commentator/analyst, he has covered many of golf's major championships on the USA Network and NBCSports.com. He is also the host for video content on the new website GolfersMD and is a weekly columnist for the *Metro NY* newspaper. In addition, Brian coproduced and appeared in *Get in the Game*, an instructional DVD for junior golfers.

Tom Mackin has worked as an associate editor at *GOLF Magazine* and as a contributing editor for *The World of Hibernia, Hudson County Magazine*, and *Zagat's America's Top Golf Courses*. A frequent contributor on golf and travel to many national and international publications, he has written for *Travel + Leisure GOLF, LINKS Magazine, NICKLAUS Magazine, Golf World, The Met Golfer, Pebble Beach Magazine, Town & Country*, the *New York Times*, and *New Jersey Monthly*. He is a native of Bayonne, New Jersey, and a graduate of Rutgers University.

Acknowledgments

Cheryl Anderson:
Special thanks to my husband, Lorin, and my parents, Henry and Geraldine, for their endless support and encouragement, and my daughter, Callie, for being the best gift that I ever have received. I'd also like to thank Fairway & Greene, Callaway Golf, and Etonic for their support and Mike Bender for sharing his vast knowledge with me. I would also like to thank my co-authors for their commitment to make *Teach Yourself VISUALLY Golf* and *Golf VISUAL Quick Tips* the best that we can make them.

Brian Crowell:
First and foremost I would like to thank my wife, Wendy, and our three amazing kids, Kevin, Casey, and Christina, for their love and understanding throughout my years in the golf business. I am also grateful for the guidance and support of my parents, Stewart and Carolyn Crowell. I also thank the members and owners of GlenArbor GC for their encouragement and for providing a gorgeous photo shoot location for this book. I would also like to recognize Mark Vassalotti, Kathy Colwell, and the many representatives of Nike Golf for providing me with awesome equipment. A special thank you to Lorin Anderson, who recommended me for this project and gave me the opportunity to work with my two amazing co-authors.

   I would also like to take this opportunity to highlight a number of people who have had a very positive impact on my career. Thanks to Paul Radetsky, Pete and Rich Shea, Will Fenn, Jim Dwyer, Jim O'Mara, Mark Jeffers of MarSar Productions, Tom Carter of GolfersMD, Paul Wilson, John Steinbreder, Jon Miller, Tommy Roy, Mike Breed, Mike Cherrone, and Mark Zimmerman and Brian Jacobs of Headline Media. Tom Kraly, however, has done nothing to inspire me.

   Finally, I want to thank Pam Mourouzis and the entire staff at Wiley Publishing for the effort and expertise required to make this book a success.

Tom Mackin:
I'd like to thank Lorin Anderson and Marilyn Allen for bringing me to this project, Cheryl Anderson and Brian Crowell for sharing their knowledge and patiently answering endless questions, Fred Vuich and Michael Cohen for getting the pictures, and Pam Mourouzis and the Wiley staff for making it all happen. I'd also like to dedicate my effort with love and thanks to my parents, Tom Mackin, Sr., and Mary Mackin, for introducing me to golf and encouraging me to follow my dreams, and to my uncle Peter McVeigh for taking me out on my first 18-hole course and showing me the way to play.

Table of Contents

1

Equipment   2

Clubs 4

Balls and Tees 12

Club Distance Charts 14

2

Warming Up   16

Stretch 18

Use the Practice Areas 22

Practice with a Purpose 24

3

Getting Set: Your Grip and Stance   26

Grip the Club 28

Find the Right Grip Pressure 31

Choose a Type of Grip 32

Position Your Hands. 34

Assume Your Stance. 36

Position the Ball 39

Align Your Shot. 40

Square the Clubface. 43

4 Driving 44

Tee It Up 46

Use the Tee Box 47

Keys to the Driver Swing 49

Make the Swing 50

Driver or Not? 55

Tee Shot Routine 56

5 The Iron Swing 58

Ball Position 60

Balance and Posture 61

Practice Swing 62

Backswing 63

Downswing 68

Impact 69

Follow-Through 71

Finish 72

Swing Path 73

6 Tricky Lies 76

Hit Out of a Divot 78

Hit from Up Against the Collar 79

Hit Out of Deep Rough 80

Hit Out from Under a Tree 82

Hit Off a Sidehill Lie 83

Hit Off a Downhill Lie 85

Hit Off an Uphill Lie 86

Chipping and Pitching 88

What Is Chipping? 90

Chipping Stance 91

Chipping Swing 92

Chipping from the Fairway 93

Chipping from the Rough 94

What Is Pitching? 95

Pitching Stance 96

Pitching Swing. 100

Bunker Shots 102

Hit Out of a Greenside Bunker 104

Hit Out of a Fairway Bunker. 110

Handle Various Bunker Lies. 111

Putting 114

Putting Routine 116

Grip the Putter 119

Take Your Stance. 121

Make the Swing 125

Read the Green. 127

Control the Distance. 129

10 Troubleshooting 132

Fix a Slice. 134

Fix a Hook 139

Avoid Hitting Fat Shots 142

Avoid Hitting Thin or Topping 144

Stop Hitting Pop-Ups 146

Stop Hitting Line Drives 147

11 Drills 148

Driver Drills 150

Iron Drills 154

Chipping/Pitching Drills 159

Bunker Drills 163

Putting Drills 166

12 Review the Rules 170

Yellow Stakes 172

Red Stakes 173

White Stakes 174

Lost and Found 175

On the Green 176

In a Bunker 177

Obstructions 178

Essential Golf Etiquette. 180

Keep Score 184

Games You Can Play   **186**

Glossary   **188**

Index   **201**

chapter **1**

Equipment

No piece of golf equipment is more important than the clubs you use to hit the ball. There are all sorts of cool gadgets and accessories to consider, but you can't do anything on the course without clubs. This chapter discusses all the clubs you will need and their purposes, plus the different types of balls and tees available.

Clubs **4**

Balls and Tees. **12**

Club Distance Charts **14**

Clubs

Golf clubs differ in size, shape, and purpose. Each club is designed to hit the ball a certain yardage—a distance that is affected by many factors. This section discusses the parts of a golf club and the types of clubs you should include in your bag.

PARTS OF A GOLF CLUB

A golf club is made up of three main components: the grip, shaft, and clubhead.

The *grip* is your physical connection to the club. Made of different materials, including rubber and leather, grips are designed to enable you to maintain your hold on the club throughout your swing.

The *shaft* of a golf club is made primarily of steel or graphite. Steel is usually used for irons and wedges, while graphite, which is lighter, is used mostly for drivers and woods to promote higher swing speeds.

The *clubhead* is the part of the club that strikes the ball. Your goal is to hit the ball with the center, or "sweet spot," of the clubface, but you might hit the ball off the *heel* (the end closer to the shaft) or the *toe* (the end farther from the shaft). The *hosel* connects the clubhead to the shaft.

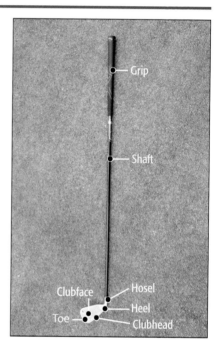

Grip

Shaft

Clubface

Toe

Hosel

Heel

Clubhead

DRIVER

The *driver* is the longest club and has the largest clubhead of all the clubs in your bag. It also hits the ball the farthest when swung properly.

Drivers, which are almost always used to hit the ball off the tee, vary in length, clubhead size, and *loft* (angle of the clubface). Although many professional golfers use a driver with a loft of less than 10 degrees, beginners should consider a driver with a greater loft, which will help you get the ball into the air more easily. In general, men should look for a loft of 9.5 to 12.0 degrees, and women 12.0 to 15.5 degrees.

As for the driver's clubhead size, the bigger the better. Having a large clubface reduces your margin of error when you hit the ball less than perfectly; even shots struck off-center tend to go farther and somewhat straighter than in the past, when clubheads were smaller.

CONTINUED ON NEXT PAGE

FAIRWAY WOODS

Fairway woods look similar to drivers. The main differences are the size of the clubhead (fairway woods are smaller) and the loft of the clubface (fairway woods have a higher degree of loft). Although most woods today have clubheads made of metal, they're called *woods* because the clubheads used to be made of wood; they are sometimes referred to as *metal woods*.

Woods come in numbers that ascend according to the amount of loft of the clubface: 2-wood, 3-wood, 4-wood, 5-wood, 7-wood, and 9-wood. The higher the number, the more loft the club has, and the more loft it has, the higher and shorter the ball should travel when hit properly. A basic set of woods usually includes a driver, a 3-wood, and a 5-wood.

TIP

Keep protective head covers on both your driver and your fairway woods to help prevent the clubfaces and their longer shafts from being damaged while in your bag.

IRONS

Irons have a completely different shape and size of clubhead than drivers and woods. They are numbered in an ascending order (from 1 to 9) that corresponds to the amount of loft of the clubface. The more loft an iron has, the shorter the distance your shot should travel. A basic set of irons usually includes irons 3 through 9.

Iron clubheads come in a variety of types, including:

- **Forged:** A block of solid metal is shaved down to form this club. This detailed process usually makes forged irons the most expensive type.
- **Cast:** Metal is poured into a mold to make this club, allowing a wider range of shapes to be used.
- **Offset:** The term *offset* describes the point at which the shaft joins the clubhead: The leading edge of this club is slightly behind the hosel. Offset irons are highly recommended for beginners because they help keep the hands in proper position at impact.
- **Cavity-back:** This type of iron has a space carved out just behind the clubface, allowing more weight to be distributed around the perimeter of the club. This extra weight makes the iron more forgiving of off-center hits by creating a larger sweet spot.

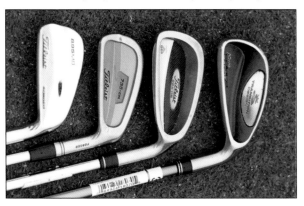

TIP

A starter set of irons should be offset with a cavity back and a low center of gravity. The offset design of the shaft will help you visually when aiming the club as well as keep your hands ahead of the ball. The cavity-back design and low center of gravity will make the ball fly higher when struck properly.

HYBRIDS

An increasing number of professional and amateur golfers are replacing the 3-iron and 4-iron with a new type of club called a *hybrid.* Hybrid clubs blend the properties of a wood and an iron and help you get the ball up into the air more effectively than low-numbered irons do. Because hybrids have longer shafts than irons, you can generate more swing speed and more distance. A selection of hybrids, which vary by degree of loft, are available, although each manufacturer labels its products differently—unlike irons, which are always identified by the same numbers. When purchasing a new set of clubs, we recommend that you substitute hybrids, which can be purchased separately, for the 3- and 4-irons.

TIP

Hybrids can also be used for approach shots around the green. See Chapter 7 for more information.

WEDGES

Wedges are the clubs with the highest amount of loft. You use them for approach shots to the green, whether you are in the fairway, rough, or sand. Because of their loft, these clubs add height to a shot, as well as impart spin on the ball due to the angle at which the clubface strikes the ball.

Many types are available, including the *pitching wedge, gap wedge, sand wedge,* and *lob wedge,* in ascending order of loft on the clubface. As with woods, the degree of loft determines how high in the air the ball will go: The greater the degree of loft, the higher the ball will go when struck properly.

A starter set of golf clubs usually includes a pitching wedge and a sand wedge. A standard pitching wedge has a loft of 48 degrees, while a standard sand wedge has a 54- to 57-degree loft. As your ability to control the distance of your shots improves, consider purchasing additional wedges with different lofts (i.e., 52, 56, 58, and 60 degrees) that you can use for particular yardages.

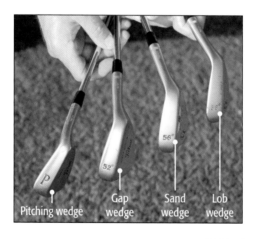

CONTINUED ON NEXT PAGE

PUTTER

Your goal in golf is to get the ball into the hole, and the club that almost always does that is the putter. Although you need only one putter in your bag, this club comes in many different shapes and sizes. From top to bottom:

- **Odyssey Two Ball:** Features white circles directly behind the clubface to help you align putts visually.

- **Classic:** Offers a sightline right behind the clubface; the heel and toe are weighted to promote a smooth, balanced stroke.

- **Futura:** Helps distribute weight behind the clubface, which helps you balance the club through the putting stroke.

- **Blade:** Has a very small sweet spot on the clubface, making it hard for beginners to use.

- **Scotty Cameron Detour:** Contains a visual element, such as a curving extension behind the clubface, to promote an inside-square-inside swing path (see "Swing Path" in Chapter 5).

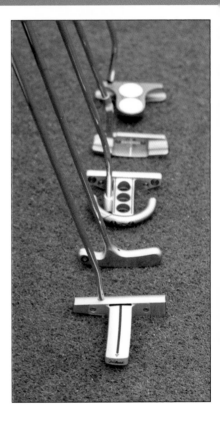

GOLF CLUB MAINTENANCE

Like your golf swing, you need to maintain and inspect your clubs to make sure that they are in proper condition. Two parts of every club—the grip and the clubface—need particular attention.

Grips wear out over time, so it's important to have them replaced as needed—ideally once a year. Do so at the beginning of your golf season to start fresh. Golf stores often offer grip replacement services; you can also take your clubs to a club professional.

Having a towel in your golf bag is important in both poor and fair weather. You can use it to dry the grips of your clubs and to remove dirt, grass, and sand from the clubface. A clean clubface is important because those materials can affect the amount of spin put on the ball after it's struck. Try to clean your clubs after every round to help reduce wear and tear.

TIP

Your height and build affect the type and length of club that best suits you. A PGA or LPGA professional can arrange a club-fitting session, during which your body is measured in relation to a golf club and your swing is analyzed (usually on video) to gauge the speed of your swing and the typical path along which your shots travel. This information enables the professional to recommend the appropriate length, shaft type, and *lie angle* (the angle between the center of the shaft and the sole of the club when it is flat on the ground) of clubs, including putters, for you.

Balls and Tees

With top-of-the-line golf clubs in your bag, you can take an enjoyable walk around the course, but you can't play golf. To do that, you need to purchase golf balls and tees on which to place them.

BALLS

There are almost as many brands of golf balls as there are golf clubs. The two basic types are:

- **Hard:** Built for more distance with a firmer feel, this type of ball is the cheaper of the two.
- **Soft:** Considered softer because of the materials used in it and its thinner outer layer, this type of ball enables golfers to impart more spin.

You can try both types to see which plays better for you, but in general, beginners should consider buying the harder balls. Their lower spin rate can help reduce the likelihood of off-target shots while you learn the game.

TEES

Even golf tees vary in size, shape, and color. You will probably use a long tee when tee-ing off with a driver to ensure that the ball sits up high. Shorter tees are used for iron, hybrid, and wedge shots, when you want the ball closer to the ground. Other tees, such as the brush tee pictured here, are available in various materials or designs to promote improved contact between the clubface and the ball.

Note: *If you play in a competition, check with the rules official about the regulations regarding tees. Tees other than the standard short and long ones might not be allowed.*

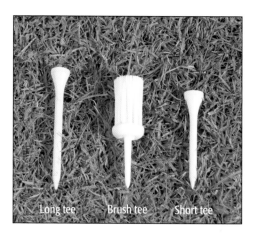

Long tee   Brush tee   Short tee

TIP

Running out of tees? Next time you play, check in and around each tee box for per-fectly good tees left behind by other players. Even the top part of a tee that's been broken in half can be used again for a low tee shot.

Club Distance Charts

How far *you* hit the ball depends on many factors—how hard you swing, how the club-face meets the ball at impact, weather and course conditions, etc.—but the following table gives you a general idea of how far each club can hit a ball on average.

Club Distance Chart		
Club	*Men's Average Distance*	*Women's Average Distance*
Driver	225+ yards	180+ yards
3-wood	210 yards	170 yards
5-wood	190 yards	160 yards
7-wood	—	150 yards
9-wood	—	140 yards
3-hybrid	180 yards	—
4-iron/4-hybrid	170 yards	135 yards
5-iron/5-hybrid	160 yards	125 yards
6-iron	150 yards	110 yards
7-iron	140 yards	100 yards
8-iron	125 yards	90 yards
9-iron	115 yards	80 yards
Pitching wedge	95 yards	70 yards
Sand wedge	75 yards	50 yards
Lob wedge	50 yards	—

Knowing how far you can hit the ball with each club is crucial to your accuracy and decision making on the course. While the table on the opposite page lists average distances for golfers in general, how far *you* hit the ball might vary widely from those numbers—every golfer is different. If you know your own game and your own distances, you are likely to make better club selections.

Bring the chart below with you the next time you go to the driving range or play a course. Write down the yardages you hit for each club so that you can refer to the chart in your following rounds.

My Club Distance Chart	
Club	*My Average Distance*
Driver	
3-wood	
5-wood	
7-wood	
9-wood	
3-hybrid	
4-iron/4-hybrid	
5-iron/5-hybrid	
6-iron	
7-iron	
8-iron	
9-iron	
Pitching wedge	
Sand wedge	
Lob wedge	
Other	

2

Warming Up

Whether you hit a few practice putts or work through a bucket of balls on the practice range, warming up gets you ready to play. It loosens your muscles, which helps prevent injury and improves your ability to make a proper swing. Back and wrist injuries are the most common among golfers, especially women because of their smaller wrists.

Stretching the muscles you will use while playing golf—primarily your back, shoulder, and leg muscles—is also important. In fact, stretching for five minutes before a round is more important than hitting balls on the range for the same amount of time.

Stretch **18**

Use the Practice Areas **22**

Practice with a Purpose **24**

Stretch

Today, there are golf-specific exercise therapists who can build an individualized program for you. Short of going to that expense, you can do these basic stretches prior to play (and even during a round) to warm up and stay loose.

This stretch helps improve your balance and stability during the swing. Hold onto a cart or other stable object with your right hand and grasp your left foot or ankle with your left hand. Bring that foot up toward your posterior until you feel a stretch in your thigh, hamstring, and hip. Hold for 15 seconds and then repeat with the opposite hand and leg.

This stretch works on the muscles in and around the hips, which will help with your hip rotation during the swing. Sit on a golf cart (or on the edge of a chair or bench) and place your right ankle on top of your left knee. With your right palm, gently push down on your right knee and hold for 15 seconds. Repeat with the opposite leg and hand.

This stretch helps you maintain stability and improves your posture throughout the swing.

1. Standing next to a golf cart, place your right heel on the floor of the cart, with your toes pointing upward.

2. Bend from the hips and reach toward your toes with your right hand. Hold that position for 15 seconds to feel a stretch in your calf and hamstring.

3. Repeat with the opposite leg and hand.

Tight shoulders can lead to poor posture and a faulty swing path that forces the club to come over the top of the ball. This stretch targets the rotator cuff area and will help you rotate your shoulders properly.

1. Hold one end of a club with your left palm facing downward, as shown.

2. Grasp the other end of the club with your right palm facing upward. The club should point upward underneath your right shoulder.

3. Gently pull up with your left hand and hold the stretch for 15 seconds.

4. Repeat under the other shoulder, reversing the positions of your hands.

CONTINUED ON NEXT PAGE

This torso exercise helps with trunk rotation by stretching the large muscles in your back. A lack of trunk flexibility can lead to improper swing mechanics and possibly even back injury.

1 Hold a club straight out in front of you, pointing outward from your chest. Grip the club as far down the shaft as is comfortable.

2 Slowly turn to the right as far as you can.

3 Return to center and then slowly turn to the left.

This side stretch helps improve your ability to rotate your body through the swing. Hold a club at opposite ends over your head. Lean to one side and hold for 15 seconds, stretching your oblique and shoulder muscles. Return to vertical and then repeat on the other side.

If you're using a golf cart, grab hold of the back of it and bend forward at the hips, pressing backward with your rear end. Hold for 15 seconds. This overall body stretch will help loosen up your shoulders, back, arms, hips, and legs.

Virtually every golf course has a practice putting green just outside the clubhouse or near the first tee. Here you can hit some putts while waiting for the starter to call your group. Keep in mind that this area is often used solely for putting; don't hit chip shots onto the green unless it is permitted.

Try two types of putts before your round—long ones (around 40 feet) and short ones (around 10 feet)—to get a feel for the pace of the greens. Always finish by making a few putts to begin the round with confidence.

Many courses also offer a driving range where you can practice hitting balls. You hit off mats or real grass toward targets in the distance. Check the yardage to each target so that you can accurately gauge how far you are hitting the ball.

You can obtain a bucket of practice range balls (the cost of which is sometimes included in your green fee; otherwise, you must pay for it separately) either in the pro shop or via a machine near the driving range. Some pro shops will provide a token needed to obtain practice balls at the machine. Don't worry about picking up the balls after you hit them; the range has a vehicle that picks up all the balls. In fact, don't walk forward onto the range from the designated hitting area to grab an extra ball to hit; it's not worth the potential physical danger.

Hitting buckets of balls for hours on end at the driving range can be fun, but will it help your golf game? Probably not. Practicing *with a purpose* will make you a better player. First, stretch for a few minutes before you hit any balls. If you are not focusing on anything specific, start with your wedges and work on your swing tempo without worrying about distance. Then work your way up through your clubs, eventually getting to your driver. End the practice session by hitting some more wedge shots to develop your touch and feel.

USE TARGETS

Hitting ball after ball at nothing in particular will not help you make more accurate shots on the course, where your goal is to get the ball *into the hole*. That's why most practice ranges have greens with colored flags that serve as targets. Find out the distance to each flag so that you can determine what club you need to use to reach that distance. You don't need flags to aim at, though; aim for a shadow or patch of discolored grass in the distance, or hit your first ball and then use that ball as your target.

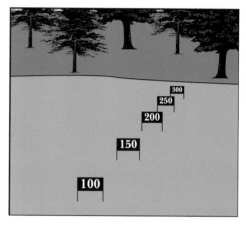

HIT ALL ODDS OR EVENS

Hitting practice shots with every club in your bag will only tire you out. Instead, select a few clubs to work with in each session. For example, devote a practice session to your even-numbered irons (pitching wedge, 8-iron, and 6-iron) and get a feel for hitting different shots.

PLAY HOLES

Set aside ten balls for the end of your practice session and hit them as if you were playing the first three holes of the next course you will play. Visualize each hole and practice as if you were executing each shot on that hole. Wait 30 seconds or so between shots to help re-create the feel of being on the course, where you would be walking or riding to your next shot.

WORK ON YOUR SHORT GAME

The majority of shots you take on a golf course are from 100 yards and in, so devote a practice session to using only your wedges. The better feel you have for these clubs, the better you will be able to get the ball close to the hole and improve your scores.

3

Getting Set:
Your Grip and Stance

Learning how to hold the club may be the single most important lesson in golf, because your grip affects both the power and the accuracy of your shots. This chapter discusses the steps to making a proper grip and the different types of grips you can use, as well as the proper stance and alignment you should assume to begin your swing.

Grip the Club **28**

Find the Right Grip Pressure. **31**

Choose a Type of Grip **32**

Position Your Hands **34**

Assume Your Stance **36**

Position the Ball. **39**

Align Your Shot **40**

Square the Clubface **43**

A good grip is essential to a sound swing. Building a proper grip is a two-step process that involves the placement of your left hand and then the placement of your right hand on the club (or the opposite sequence for left-handers).

LEFT HAND

1 Take hold of the club with your left hand. The club should touch the two points indicated by the Xs in the photo, with your left index finger and the opposite side of your palm's heel pad touching the grip.

Assuming the proper grip with your left hand enables you to hold the club in the air simply by curling your left index finger around the club.

TIP

When it comes to the grips on your clubs, the number of options has never been greater. All sorts of styles and colors are available, with varying textures, thicknesses, and degrees of cushioning. Try a variety of styles to determine which one is most comfortable for your hands.

2 Close your left hand around the club. Your thumb and index finger should form a V-shape, as shown here. The bottom of this V should point toward your right shoulder.

3 Maintaining this grip with your left hand, bend your wrist toward you to lift the club straight up into the air. In a standard (or *neutral*) grip, you should see two knuckles on the left side of the shaft, and your thumb should rest on the right side of center on the shaft.

FAQ

How should I care for my grips?

Ideally, you should have a professional replace your grips at least once a year; do so at the beginning of the season for a fresh start. Periodically clean your grips with dish soap and water, and then let them dry thoroughly.

CONTINUED ON NEXT PAGE

RIGHT HAND

With your left hand on the club, place your right hand directly below it, resting naturally on the club. The exact placement of the right hand's fingers will depend on the type of grip you choose (see pages 32–33).

With both hands on the club, the center of your right palm will rest directly on top of your left thumb. Your left thumb should rest against the lifeline of your right palm, as shown. Your right index finger should be separated from your middle finger and curved around the grip as if you were pulling the trigger on a gun.

Trigger finger

The thumb and forefinger of each hand should form a V-shape. Your best chance of hitting the ball straight is to ensure that the bottom of each V is pointing toward your right shoulder. If the Vs are facing right of that point, your clubface will tend to be closed at impact (see "Square the Clubface" on page 43), and your shot will likely go low and to the left. If the Vs are facing left of your right shoulder, your club-face will tend to be open at impact, and the ball will likely go to the right.

Find the Right Grip Pressure

The amount of pressure you exert with your grip affects your ability to make a good swing. Gripping the club too tightly will tense your arm muscles and limit your club speed. If you grip the club too loosely, you will lose control of the clubhead and your accuracy will suffer. A good grip pressure is the same pressure you would use when holding a child's hand. The grip pressure of your left hand comes mainly from the middle, ring, and pinky fingers. On your right hand, the index finger, middle finger, and thumb supply the pressure.

MAINTAIN CONSISTENT GRIP PRESSURE

Maintain consistent grip pressure throughout the swing. A poor grip can't keep hold of two tees (as shown in the photo), especially if there is too much space between the right thumb and forefinger. That will lead you to either change grip pressure during the swing or overswing, because the shaft will drop in your hands at the top of the backswing.

MATCH YOUR GRIP PRESSURE TO YOUR SHOT

Different situations call for different levels of grip pressure. For example, hitting a ball out of heavy rough requires a firmer grip than hitting a ball off the fairway. This table gives you some guidelines for adjusting your grip pressure to the shot you're facing, with 1 representing the loosest grip and 10 representing the tightest grip.

Situation	Grip Pressure
Short pitch (a high, soft shot)	3
Fairway shot	6
Shot out of heavy rough	8

TIP

Hold a club straight out in front of you and ask someone to try to pull it out of your hands. If your grip pressure is too loose, he will be able to yank it away easily. If he can't move the club at all, your grip pressure is too tight. If the club moves slightly forward in your hands but does not come completely out, your grip pressure is just right.

Golfers use multiple types of grips. Choose the one that feels the most comfortable to you.

OVERLAPPING

In the *overlapping grip,* the pinky of your right hand rests on top of the space between the index and middle fingers of your left hand. We recommend this grip because it promotes a feeling of connection between the hands and the club.

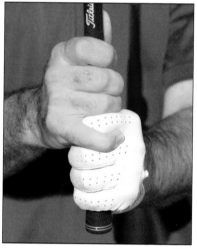

INTERLOCKING

In the *interlocking grip,* you interlace the pinky of your right hand and the index finger of your left hand. Golfers with small hands and fingers should consider the interlocking or baseball grip for a better hold on the club.

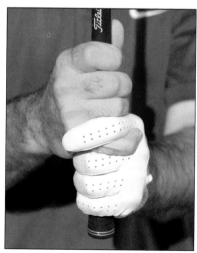

BASEBALL

With the baseball grip, also known as the *ten-finger grip,* all ten of your fingers touch the club, and your left thumb is covered by the base of your right thumb.

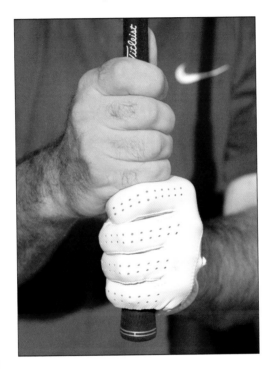

TIP

Small hands and fingers can make gripping the club a bit more difficult. First, make sure that your grips on your clubs are the right size for your hands. Then try the baseball grip, where all ten fingers are on the club. This grip might feel more comfortable and secure to you than interlocking or overlapping your right pinky.

Within each of the three grip types are different hand placements that affect the position of the clubface when it hits the ball. A neutral grip is ideal for most golfers. As your skills improve, you can experiment with strong and weak grips to hit draw shots and fade shots (see pages 41–42 for more information), respectively.

WEAK

With a weak grip, you can see less than two knuckles on your left hand and one or two on your right hand. The Vs formed by your hands point toward your left shoulder. With this grip, the clubface can be open at impact, possibly leading to a fade or a slice.

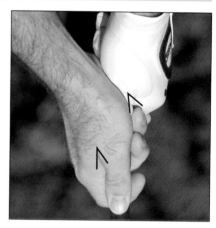

STRONG

With a strong grip, you see three knuckles on your left hand and one or none on your right. The Vs formed by your hands point toward the outside of your right shoulder. With this grip, the clubface can be closed at impact, possibly leading to a draw or a hook.

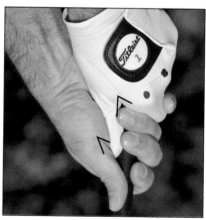

NEUTRAL

With a neutral grip, you can see one or two knuckles on your left hand and one knuckle on your right hand. The Vs formed by your hands point toward your right shoulder. With this grip, the clubface can be square (see page 43) at impact, usually creating a straight shot.

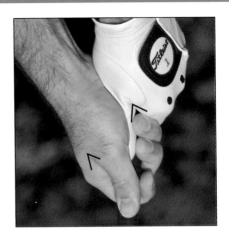

TIP

Many beginners tend to hit the ball to the right. A short-term solution to that problem is to create a stronger grip by rotating your left hand to the right after you place it on the club. When you do so, you will see two to three knuckles on your left hand and one knuckle on your right hand. Keep in mind, though, that strengthening your grip can lead to the opposite problem: shots that pull to the left. See Chapter 10 for help in straightening out your swing.

Once you have established your grip, you need to stand in the proper position. To finish your swing in balance, you must begin your swing in balance. If you don't, your body will try to rebalance itself during the swing, throwing your weight shift and clubhead position out of whack. A balanced stance is also easier to repeat and involves less unnecessary motion.

TIP

When you're in the proper stance, you should feel as if you're standing on the edge of a swimming pool getting ready to dive into the water.

Your stance will be almost identical for every full-swing shot, so establish a comfortable position that you can repeat over and over. When chipping, hitting bunker shots, or putting, you will alter your stance, but in general you should:

- Bend forward from the hips.

- Flex your knees slightly.

- Keep your back straight, without any arch.

- Tilt your spine slightly to the right to raise your left shoulder above your right shoulder.

- Let your hands hang directly beneath your shoulders.

- Point the grip end of the club between your belly button and belt buckle.

- Keep your feet parallel to one another unless you are setting up to hit a draw or fade (see pages 41–42).

- Distribute your weight evenly between your feet and concentrate it in the area underneath your shoelaces, not on your toes or heels.

CONTINUED ON NEXT PAGE

Here are two examples of what you should *not* be doing in your stance:

- Reaching out to the ball with your arms overextended. Overextending your arms puts most of your weight over your toes, leading to an unbalanced swing.

- Standing too upright and rigid without any knee flex. This creates tension that prevents your shoulders from making a good turn. It also creates a downswing that is too steep, which can cause you to top the ball or hit too far beneath the ball.

TIP

To practice your stance, stand in front of a mirror as if you were hitting into it. Look to make sure that your feet, shoulders, forearms, and knees are aligned together. If you placed a golf club straight across each pair of those body parts, it should point in a direction parallel to where you want the ball to go.

While your stance remains essentially the same for most swings, the position of the ball within your stance will change depending on the club you are using.

The distance between you and the ball is determined by the length of the club you are using. The longer the club, the farther you will stand from the ball. Your arms should hang naturally from your shoulders, without you having to reach out toward the ball.

The longer the club you are using, the more toward the front of your stance you should position the ball. The ball ideally should be positioned at the point where your swing bottoms out. The longer the club, the farther forward in your stance that point will be.

TIP

Follow these general guidelines when positioning the ball between your feet:

- **Driver and woods:** Forward in your stance, off the inside of your left heel.
- **Irons and hybrids:** Nearer to the center of your stance.
- **Wedges:** Slightly right of center.

The way you line up to hit the ball is as important as the swing you make. Altering your stance will affect the path the ball takes after leaving the clubface.

Before every shot, you must select a target. It could be the flagstick, a particular area of the green, or a spot on the fairway. As you place your club behind the ball, make sure that the clubface is pointed at your target, and then take your stance. Imagine that you're standing on railroad tracks, your feet and body on one rail, the ball and clubhead on the other.

TIP

While your clubface is aimed at the target, your shoulders, hips, and feet should naturally point just left of the target. If your feet are pointing directly at the target, then your ball and clubface are pointing to the right of the target. Most golfers aim too far to the right and then compensate by swinging their arms too far to the left, usually creating a shot that begins on a path far left of your target.

DRAW SHOTS

A shot that moves gradually from right to left is called a *draw*. To hit a draw shot, you must angle your feet so that a line drawn across your toes points to the right of the target. This stance will produce an inside-out swing, imparting spin on the ball that will make it curve to the left. (See Chapter 5 for more on inside-out swings.)

CONTINUED ON NEXT PAGE

FADE SHOTS

A shot that moves gradually from left to right in a controlled manner is called a *fade.* To hit a fade shot, you must angle your feet so that your line points to the left of the target. This stance will produce an outside-in swing, imparting spin on the ball that will make it curve to the right. (See "Swing Path" in Chapter 5 for more on outside-in swings.)

FAQ

Why would I want to hit a draw or fade on purpose?

As your skills improve, so too will your ability to shape the flight path of your ball. Suppose your ball comes to rest behind a tree in the fairway. If the pin is on the far right side of the green, you want to hit a fade that curves around the tree from left to right and rolls toward the hole. If the pin is on the far left side of the green, you want to hit a draw from right to left toward the hole.

Just as your stance affects the direction of the ball, so too does the position of the clubface when it strikes the ball.

A *square clubface* will likely produce a straight shot. Focus on lining the leading edge of the iron up to the ball so that it is perpendicular to your target line.

An *open clubface* will likely produce a fade or slice shot that curves to the right.

A *closed clubface* will likely produce a draw or hook shot that curves to the left.

Driving

There may be no better feeling on the golf course than hitting a perfect drive and watching it soar down the fairway. To achieve this result, you need to have certain fundamentals in place. This chapter describes the process of using your driver (and some alternative clubs) on the tee: using the tee box to your advantage, teeing the ball up correctly, and making a properly balanced swing.

Tee It Up 46

Use the Tee Box 47

Keys to the Driver Swing. 49

Make the Swing 50

Driver or Not? 55

Tee Shot Routine 56

Driving the ball successfully begins before you take the club in your hand. A driver has the largest head of any club, so you must tee up the ball properly.

Because your driver has the largest clubface of any club, and because it should make contact with the ball on a slight upswing, you need to tee the ball up higher than you would with any other club. Use a longer tee, as shown here.

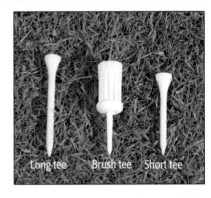

Long tee   Brush tee   Short tee

By putting the ball on the tee just above where the clubface sits when you address the ball, you will be able to strike the ball on a slight upswing, ideally in the center of the clubface.

TIP

In some instances, you should tee the ball lower when using a driver, such as when you are hitting into a strong wind (you want the ball to fly lower to reduce the wind's effect). If you have a steep downswing, which makes the club come at the ball at a sharp angle, teeing it lower helps you avoid hitting underneath the ball, which produces a pop-up into the air without much distance.

Every hole on the course has a *tee box*—an area defined by two markers that indicate where you can tee up your first shot. It's illegal to tee the ball up in front of or outside these markers; if you do so during an official competition, you will incur a penalty. However, if your ball is within the defined tee box area, your feet can be outside the markers as you take your tee shot.

To hole ———→

You are allowed to tee the ball anywhere between the two markers and as far as two club lengths back from each of the markers, as shown here.

CONTINUED ON NEXT PAGE

You can use the tee box to your advantage by working with the shape of the fairway and the natural shape of your shot. For example, if you're aiming for a fairway that has water or bunkers on the right side and you naturally *slice* the ball (curving from left to right in an uncontrolled manner), tee up your ball on the right side of the tee box. Doing so will make the fairway "wider" visually, enabling you to start the ball's flight away from the hazard and giving you confidence that you can land the ball away from the hazard.

TIP

At some courses, not all tee boxes are directly parallel to the fairway. On each hole, make sure that you choose a target and line yourself up with that target rather than lining up parallel to the tee box itself.

Keys to the Driver Swing

To execute a good swing with a driver, you must:

- Make sure that your left shoulder starts slightly higher than your right (which should happen naturally because your right hand is lower on the club than your left).

- Keep your head behind the ball from the start of the swing until just after impact.

- Put 60 percent of your weight on your right foot because the ball is forward in your stance and the ball is on a tee. Doing so mimics the desired position at impact.

Because the driver is the longest club you will own (other than a long putter), the swing you make with it will be wider and longer than any other. Your goal for driving should be solid contact between the clubface and the ball, which leads to a good blend of accuracy and distance.

STANCE

Position the ball off the inside of your left heel. Your head should be just behind the ball, but your hands need to be directly in line with the ball. Your grip (with your right hand below your left) should tilt your shoulders so that your left shoulder is slightly higher than your right one. Your feet should be shoulder width apart.

Head behind ball

Left shoulder higher than right

Hands in line with ball

60% of weight on right foot

Feet shoulder width apart

TIP

If your head is positioned in front of the ball, one of two things is likely to happen: Your downswing will be too steep, leading to a fat or popped-up shot, or the clubface will be open at impact, likely leading to a slice.

BEGINNING OF SWING

To begin your swing, turn your hands, arms, shoulders, and the clubhead back and inside away from the ball, and start to hinge your wrists.

HALFWAY BACK

As you continue to move the club back, hinge your wrists more as your hands move past your right hip. The club should be at a 45-degree angle to your right hip, with your weight slowly moving into your right heel.

TIP

To feel a proper wrist hinge, grip a club and hold it straight out in front of you. Then bend your wrists toward you so that the club points straight up in the air (your thumbs should be pointing toward the sky).

CONTINUED ON NEXT PAGE

TOP OF BACKSWING

At the top of your backswing, the shaft of the club should be roughly parallel to the ground. That depends on your own range of motion—more flexible golfers could take the shaft past parallel, while less flexible golfers might not be able to reach parallel. Ideally, your left arm at this point should be as long as it was when you set up to the ball. Your left shoulder should be behind the ball to make a full turn, and the club should be pointing in the general direction of the target. Most of your weight should be toward the inside of your right heel.

START OF DOWNSWING

As you begin your downswing, you should feel as if the center of your body is unwinding while your head stays back. The grip end of the club should be moving downward along an inside path toward the ball, and your weight should start moving into your left foot.

As you reach this position, your hands will be driving the grip end of the club to the ball. Notice that the clubhead is lagging behind your hands and your knees are still facing the ball.

IMPACT

At impact, your head should be behind the club. Your left arm, your left shoulder, and the club should form a straight line coming up from the ball. The inside of your right foot should still be on the ground, and your hips and belt buckle should have rotated toward the target.

HALFWAY THROUGH

Just after impact, the club should be pointing toward the target. Your right heel will be coming up off the ground, and your right wrist will have rolled over your left wrist.

TIP

Fully extending your arms at impact is an important key to distance. As a visual reminder to fully extend your arms through impact, picture another ball positioned a foot in front of the ball you are hitting. Then imagine hitting that second ball as well.

CONTINUED ON NEXT PAGE

FINISH

At the finish, all your weight should be over your left heel. Your right shoulder should be lower than your left, as when you started the swing. The shaft of the club should be right behind your neck. Your right heel will be up in the air, with only the right toe touching the ground, and your belt buckle should be pointing toward the target. (This depends on your flexibility: It could point more left if you have a greater range of motion, or more right if you are less flexible.)

TIP

A balanced finish is critical to a good swing. To work on your finish, close your eyes for an entire practice swing and hold the finish position for five seconds without opening your eyes. Being able to do so without wavering from this position is a good indication of your ability to make a balanced swing.

9.5°

Titleist

PRO·TITANIUM 905R

To see whether you have struck the ball on the proper part of the clubface, check the underside of your driver. Many times, a painted tee will leave a mark. That mark indicates where the club hit the tee, giving you a good idea of how close to the center of the clubhead you managed to strike the ball.

Driver or Not?

On par-fours and par-fives with generous fairways, you will want to use a driver and hit the ball as far as possible. On shorter par-fours and on holes with narrower fairways, consider using a fairway wood, a hybrid club, or even an iron. You will sacrifice distance but will probably gain accuracy and improve your position for the next shot. The higher the club's loft, the less sidespin it puts on the ball, and the better chance the ball has of traveling straight.

As you weigh your options, remember:

- You want your drive to end up on a level lie in the fairway. Take into account the distance you usually hit the ball and where the shot might finish.

- Consider the position of hazards (sand, water, heavy rough, and so on) before deciding which club to use. A long shot can roll through the fairway and wind up in the rough or in a hazard.

- Few golfers can reach a par-five in two shots. Plan your tee shot with your second and third shots in mind, leaving yourself comfortable distances to hit before you reach the green.

TIP

Always tee the ball up for your first shot on a hole, whether you are using a driver, a fairway wood, a hybrid club, or an iron. Although more experienced players might not use a tee when playing a par-three, beginners should always use a tee to help get the ball into the air.

Tee Shot Routine

Because your tee shot is the first shot you take on any hole, picking a target, establishing your stance, and executing a good swing are essential to scoring well. Using the same routine every time you tee off—and for any other shot, for that matter—will help you make a consistent, repeatable swing.

① After teeing up your ball, stand behind it and look at your target. Take into account where the hazards, if any, are located. Also note your potential landing area and the distance of the next shot you would face from that point.

② As you step in to take your stance, first with your right foot and then with your left, take another look at your target to ensure that you are lined up properly.

3 As you stand over the ball, "waggle" the club—move it back and forth slightly—without touching the ball. Doing so will help ease tension in your hands and arms, helping you make a fuller, more relaxed swing.

4 Right before you begin your swing, look again at the target to visualize the ball going right at it. Then make a balanced swing and watch your ball land in the fairway!

The Iron Swing

Irons require a blend of accuracy and power. These are the clubs you use to hit onto greens. If you can drive, pitch, and putt well, you will likely play a good round of golf, but to get even better, you need to hit shots that get you closer and closer to the pin. That means getting used to your 5-iron through 9-iron via practice, which will create the consistency needed to score well.

   This chapter discusses the makeup of a basic swing: the address, backswing, downswing, and finish. While some clubs (a sand wedge, for example) and some situations (such as hitting out of deep rough or a bunker) require a specific type of swing, these basics will help you hit the majority of the iron shots you will face on the course.

Ball Position 60

Balance and Posture 61

Practice Swing 62

Backswing 63

Downswing 68

Impact 69

Follow-Through 71

Finish 72

Swing Path 73

When using an iron, position the ball between your left heel and the center of your stance. Remember that the longer the club (for example, a 5-iron is longer than a 7-iron, which in turn is longer than a 9-iron), the more forward in your stance the ball should be.

- For a 4-iron or an equivalent hybrid club, position the ball a few inches inside your left heel.
- For a 5-iron, 6-iron, or 7-iron, position the ball roughly an inch left of center.

- For an 8-iron or 9-iron, position the ball in the center of your stance.
- For a wedge, position the ball slightly behind center.

Balance and Posture

The club's length affects the width of your stance in a similar way—the longer the club, the wider your stance. Keep in mind that your heels should not be farther than shoulder width apart, nor should they be closer together than the width of your hips.

The more forward the ball is in your stance, the more your shoulders will tilt naturally from left to right. You should feel slightly more than half of your weight toward your right leg. As you change the starting position of the ball from the front of your stance to the center (as you would for a 9-iron shot as compared to a 5-iron shot), your shoulders become more level, and your weight should become more equally balanced on both legs. Your head should be just behind the ball, with your hands just ahead of the ball.

Head slightly behind ball

Shoulders tilted left to right

Hands ahead of the ball

Weight balanced equally between feet

Shaft leaning forward

Feet no wider than shoulder width apart

TIP

Posture is very important during every swing. You must allow your shoulders to turn properly; any imbalance in your posture (such as standing stiffly or slouching) prevents that rotation from occurring. Many golfers find other ways to make a bigger swing—allowing the left arm to break down at the top of the backswing, turning the head away from the ball, straightening the right knee, over-rotating the hips, or swaying with the whole body—but those short-term solutions are rarely effective in the long run.

Always take one practice swing before playing an iron shot to establish your swing tempo and visualize the shot you want to hit. Make sure that you hit the ground (but not the ball) when taking a practice swing—doing so will help you get the feel of the turf and reinforce the idea that you want to take a divot. (See Chapter 10 for more information on what divots can tell you about your swing.) Don't be afraid to hit the ground; divots are okay, and you should make one whenever the ball is on the ground (except when it's on the green). Just remember to fix your divot, either by placing the turf back in the divot or by spreading sand (usually provided in your golf cart) on the spot.

Don't panic if you miss the ground during that practice swing, though. You don't want to take too many practice swings, because that would slow down the pace of play. Just set up to the ball, look at your target, and then take your swing. Whatever your goal is—whether it's simply advancing the ball or hitting the ball onto the green—commit your thoughts to that goal during the swing.

TIP

Deciding which club to use, especially after a tee shot and before reaching the green, is tough for beginners. Over time, you will learn how far you can hit each club. If you're just beginning to play, go with a more lofted club to help you get the ball up into the air more easily.

Backswing

The purpose of the backswing is to create leverage that will build power. You turn your shoulders, your arms go up and around your body, and the club is lifted into the air. The simpler the backswing, the easier it is to repeat consistently. And a consistent backswing only enhances your chances of making a good downswing. If your backswing goes off the correct path, you will have to recover on the downswing, forcing you to rely too much on timing.

FIRST MOVE

After getting into your stance, take one more look at your target before you start your swing. As you begin the backswing, your hands, arms, and shoulders and the clubhead should be turning back and inside away from the ball, with your wrists beginning to hinge.

CONTINUED ON NEXT PAGE

HALFWAY BACK

Continue to swing the club farther back and allow your wrists to hinge. The club should be at a 45-degree angle to your left arm, and your weight should be moving slowly into your right heel. If there were water in the shaft of the club, then water would be pouring out of the grip end at this point in the swing.

If the club is parallel to the ground here, you have not hinged your wrists enough. If you don't create this hinge, then it will be difficult to generate any power.

TIP

While you are developing your swing, you might be thinking of many different things: Where's my elbow? Is my grip right? Did I shift my weight correctly? Instead, try to concentrate on one thing each time you play. For example, focus on your grip for an entire round and commit to putting the correct grip on the club even if you don't hit shots well. If you feel you need another round to correct that element, do it instead of moving on to another element of the swing. You can focus on your backswing in another round and on your follow-through another time. But you can't practice every single element of the swing at once. Think of it like building a house—you can't put the roof on until you have created a strong foundation, piece by piece.

TOP OF BACKSWING

At the top of your backswing, the shaft of the club should be roughly parallel to the ground. Your ability to reach that position depends on your range of motion: More flexible golfers can get the shaft parallel to the ground, while less flexible golfers might not be able to reach parallel—and that's okay.

If you can see the club out of the corner of your left eye at this point, you're overswinging. You might see PGA Tour pros like John Daly and Phil Mickelson bring their clubs this far back, but they are tremendously skilled golfers whose rhythm is finely tuned from hitting thousands of balls. As a beginner, building a repeatable swing within your own abilities is far more important than imitating the swing of a professional golfer.

Your left arm at this point should be as long and straight as it was at address. Your left shoulder should be behind the ball and pointed downward, and the club should be pointing in the general direction of the target. Your hips will have turned approximately 45 degrees, and your right knee will be flexed. Most of your weight should be toward the inside of your right heel.

CONTINUED ON NEXT PAGE

The clubface should be square at the top of the backswing.

If the clubface is closed, as shown here, the ball will likely move left after you hit it. Golfers compensate for this problem by swinging their arms and the club to the right of the target, but doing so leads to *pushes* (shots that veer sharply right) and hooks.

If the clubface is open, as shown here, the ball will likely move right after being struck. Golfers try to compensate for this problem by swinging their arms and the club to the left of the target, but doing so leads to *pulls* (shots that veer sharply left) and slices.

At the top of your backswing, your left wrist should be flat, while your left forearm and hand should be in line. Any bend between the left wrist and forearm means that the clubface will be either opening or closing at impact. Do you feel like you could put a ruler flat against the back of your left hand and forearm? That's the feeling you're trying to achieve here.

Your right elbow should be bent and pointing down at the ground if your body is flexible enough to reach that position; if not, it will likely point behind your body. Though not recommended, this "flying right elbow" has worked for a number of great golfers, including Jack Nicklaus.

There should also be a gap between your right elbow and your body. If your elbow is pinned against your ribcage, you have to compensate in some way on the downswing to get it away from your body and create that

Left forearm and hand in line

Right elbow bent and away from body

space. If you don't, then your swing will lack power, you will make poor contact with the ball, and the clubhead will bottom out much too soon during the swing, resulting in a fat or topped shot.

TIP

If you're struggling with iron shots, try using only your favorite club for all shots (except for sand shots and putts) on a few holes to re-establish your comfort level. Doing so will also help you get creative by forcing you to play different shots—it might even be fun!

Downswing

The *downswing*—when the club moves back toward the ball—is where the power you try to build with your backswing is unleashed. Executing the downswing properly is very important, because this is the portion of the swing that leads directly to impact with the ball.

As you begin your downswing, your weight should start moving toward your left side. Your hips will rotate to the left, turning your belly button toward the target. Your shoulders and arms will follow. If a straight line were drawn at waist level, your hands and the grip end of the club would be below it, while the clubhead would still be above it.

As the club gets closer to impact, the grip end should be pointing in the direction of the ball.

TIP

During the downswing, focus on hitting the back of the ball and then the ground. Doing so will help you compress the ball against the clubface and get the maximum distance possible. It will also create a divot, ideally one that points forward, directly at your target.

Impact

At impact, your head should be behind the club. Your left arm, your left shoulder, and the club should form almost a straight line coming up from the ball. The inside of your right foot should still be on the ground, and your hips and belt buckle should be rotating toward the target. Most of your weight should be on your left leg at this point.

TIP

If you're not sure whether you can reach the green on a par-three with a particular club, choose the next lowest lofted club (for example, a 6-iron instead of a 7-iron) and tee the ball up a club length or two behind the tee markers. Doing so helps remove the indecision, and you'll make a more confident swing.

CONTINUED ON NEXT PAGE

Special tape designed to show you where the ball makes contact with the clubface is available from most club fitters. The ball leaves a mark at the exact point of impact—heel, center, or toe. (You can also sprinkle the clubface with baby powder to get the same effect.) Driving-range balls usually leave a mark on the clubface, too, so take a look at your club after a swing to notice the impact point.

The correct impact—in the center of the clubface—feels solid and almost effortless, with no twisting of the club or vibration running up the shaft into your hands. Making solid contact is more important than attempting to achieve maximum power. You will attain maximum distance only after you learn to strike the ball with the center of the clubface.

Most golfers complain that they feel the club move in their hands during a poor swing. What they are feeling are vibrations caused by the ball when it hits the inside (heel) of the clubface, as shown here, or the outside (toe) of the clubface.

TIP

If you're hitting shots off the toe or heel, use three-quarter rather than full swings during your next practice session. (That is, take the club only three-fourths of the way back.) Doing so will help you find the center of the clubface and remind you what solid contact feels like.

Just after impact, the club should be pointing toward the target. Your right heel will come up off the ground, and your left leg will be fully extended.

TIP

Halfway through a proper follow-through, your right hand will be hip high. It should be positioned as if you were going to shake someone's hand right in front of you.

At the finish, all your weight should be over your left heel. Your right shoulder should be lower than your left, just as when you began the swing. The shaft of the club should be right behind your neck. Your right heel will be up in the air, with all spikes showing and only the toes touching the ground, and your belt buckle should point toward the target. (The belt buckle can be more to the left for those with a greater range of motion, or more to the right for those who are less flexible.)

TIP

Remember, a balanced finish is critical to a good swing. Without balance, you won't be able to repeat the swing consistently. The position might be uncomfortable when you're just beginning to play, but with practice, your body will get used to supporting your weight in that position.

Swing Path

The path along which you swing the club has a major influence on the direction your ball flies after impact. Because you move the golf club up and around your body during the swing, it is never taken back and then forward on a purely straight line—rather, it should move along an arc. Any curvature of the ball's flight path that occurs after the ball leaves the clubface is a result of the position of the clubface at impact.

PROPER PATH

In an ideal swing, the clubhead moves on an inside-square-inside path. That means that during the downswing, the clubhead moves along the inside of the target line, returns to impact (square to the ball) on the target line, and then, after the ball is struck, moves to the inside again. This path enables your body to serve as the axis of what will hopefully be a repetitive motion.

If the clubface is square at impact, the ball should move directly toward your target. If the clubface is open at impact, the ball will curve to the right; if it's closed, the ball will curve left.

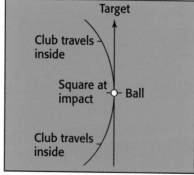

CONTINUED ON NEXT PAGE

OUTSIDE-INSIDE PATH

In an outside-inside swing path, the clubhead travels outside of the target line during the downswing so that, at impact, you are hitting across the ball to the left and then moving the clubhead sharply inside the target line. This path can result in anything from a hook to a dramatic slice, depending on the position of the clubface at impact. If it's open, it could create a massive slice back toward the target line; if closed, a dramatic hook that starts left and continues farther left could result. If the clubface is square at impact, you will likely pull the ball left.

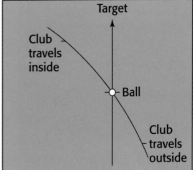

INSIDE-OUTSIDE PATH

In an inside-outside swing path, the clubhead travels back to impact from too far inside the target line; then, at impact, it continues farther out and well right of the target line. If the clubface is open at impact, the ball will start right of the target line and curve farther in that direction; if closed, the ball will start right and then curve back to the left toward the target line in a hook; and if square, the ball will be pushed straight to the right.

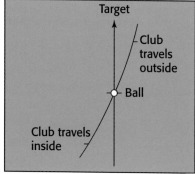

Target

Club travels outside

Ball

Club travels inside

6

Tricky Lies

In every round, your ball will come to rest in a tricky lie—in a divot, in a less-than-flat position (sidehill, downhill, or uphill), or near an impediment such as a tree, for example. Although each of these situations creates a challenge for your next shot, making some simple adjustments to your grip, stance, and ball position can improve your chances of overcoming the obstacle.

Hit Out of a Divot. **78**

Hit from Up Against the Collar. **79**

Hit Out of Deep Rough **80**

Hit Out from Under a Tree **82**

Hit Off a Sidehill Lie **83**

Hit Off a Downhill Lie **85**

Hit Off an Uphill Lie. **86**

Some golfers don't replace the divots they create in the fairway (but you should!). That means your ball might occasionally wind up on a patch of dirt—a lie that often produces a thin shot.

In this situation, you need to make sure that you feel centered in your stance. Keep your lower body stable, and do not shift your weight much, if at all, during the swing.

First, position the ball toward the back of your stance. Doing so will help you hit the ball with a descending blow. Place your hands slightly ahead of the ball with your weight favoring your left side. This will help you create an outside-to-inside swing path—more of a V-shape than the usually preferable U-shape. You want to come down at the ball at a steeper angle so that the clubhead doesn't get caught on the back edge of the divot. You also want to square the clubface to the ball's intended flight path.

As usual, your goal is to hit the ball, not the ground, first. The clubhead should reach the ball while it's still moving downward, and not on the upswing.

Occasionally, you might find your ball up against the *collar*, where the fringe of the putting surface meets the rough. You can use your putter for this shot, but you must hit the ball with a descending blow (more of a V-shaped swing) rather than the sweeping U-shaped motion you normally use for a putt. With a regular putting swing, you could miss the ball entirely because it is almost hidden by the grass.

Because you're hitting down on the ball, this shot doesn't require much of a backswing. However, you should hinge your wrists immediately and focus your eyes on the top of the ball. Your hands and arms should be very relaxed, with your weight shifted slightly left. You want to give the ball a gentle tap rather than a punch.

Keep your hands ahead of the clubhead throughout this swing. Keep in mind that the ball will roll more than usual and might jump forward immediately after impact because the grass that comes between the clubface and the ball will eliminate any back-spin.

Hit Out of Deep Rough

Just off the fairways at many golf courses lies evil grass known as *deep rough*. Balls hit into this area quickly disappear from view, nestling themselves into the tall grass to create a very difficult lie for your next shot. Deep rough is often thick enough to twist the club's hosel and close the clubface, producing an off-target shot.

Because the grass in the deep rough will come between the ball and the clubface, you have little control over where the ball might go, and the club can put little spin on the ball. This decreases accuracy and makes the ball hard to stop when it does land—a real problem if you're trying to land the ball on the green. Your goal here is simply to advance the ball to a place where you will have a better lie and therefore will be able to make a more productive swing.

Aim just left of your target and open the clubface slightly. Doing so helps offset the grass, pulling the clubface closed, and enables the club to cut through the grass better. Choke down on the club a few inches and increase your grip pressure so that you can keep hold of the club as it cuts through the rough.

You want to use an outside-to-inside swing path (see page 74) to create the steeper angle needed to hit the ball, rather than the grass behind the ball, first. This path will correspond to your stance, which should be aligned slightly left of your target. In effect, you will swing along the line created by your feet.

(see page 74)

TIP

When faced with a shot from deep rough, examine the grass. If the grass is growing in the direction of the hole, use a more lofted club, because it will slide through the grass easier, and the grass will not resist the clubhead as much. If the grass is growing away from the target, it will offer more resistance. Think more defensively in this situation and consider laying up; you're usually better off using a wedge than trying to muscle a club through deep rough that is working against you.

When your ball is under a tree whose low branches impair your swing, your main goal is to hit the ball to a spot from which you can swing comfortably. Don't try for too much—all you want is to get yourself into position for the next shot. Because the tree branches will limit the length of your swing, you will need to adjust your grip and stance.

Choke down on the club and position the ball toward your back foot. Doing so will help produce a lower-trajectory shot with more roll, helping to compensate for the abbreviated swing you will make. Your weight should be slightly forward toward your front foot.

Take some practice swings, shortening your backswing to the point where the tree branches do not interfere.

Keep your body down through the swing, matching the length of your follow-through to the length of your backswing. Don't lift your body at impact, or you will hit a thin shot.

Hit Off a Sidehill Lie

A ball on a sidehill lie is positioned either above or below your feet. Either way, the ball not being level with your feet will directly affect your stance, alignment, and swing and the direction of your shot. Because you are rarely able to practice hitting from such a lie, understanding the adjustments you need to make will make this difficult shot a bit easier.

WHEN THE BALL IS ABOVE YOUR FEET

- Use a more lofted club than you normally would for the distance, because this lie produces a right-to-left draw that will roll farther than a typical shot. If you would normally hit a 6-iron, opt for a 7-iron instead.

- Aim to the right of your target, because the uphill slope will make your shot move to the left.

- Position the ball more toward your back foot in your stance.

- Stand tall when addressing the ball, and keep your weight on the balls of your feet to help maintain balance throughout the swing.

- Grip down on the club—the steeper the incline, the farther down you should grip. Take a practice swing and hit the ground to find out how far down you need to go.

- Make a flatter swing, with your arms lower than usual at the top of the backswing. This type of swing produces a draw and the potential for hitting a fat shot. (That's why you place the ball back in your stance and aim right of your target.)

CONTINUED ON NEXT PAGE

WHEN THE BALL IS BELOW YOUR FEET

This is the most difficult lie to play from because it has the greatest potential for a topped shot. Make the following adjustments:

- Use a less lofted club than you normally would for the distance. This lie puts a side spin on the ball that results in less roll.

- Aim to the left of your target. The downward slope will produce a fade-shaped shot that moves from left to right.

- If you are hitting an 8-iron through sand wedge, place the ball in the middle of your stance; for a fairway wood, place it just left of center.

- Widen your stance and keep your weight back toward your heels to maintain your balance throughout the swing.

- Grip the club as close to the end as you can.

- Make your swing more upright than usual. Your arms and hands should go up a little higher during the backswing, and then back down to the ball. This more upright swing makes it easier to hit down on the ball and take a divot. It can also lead to an open clubface, which is why you want to aim left of the target.

When the ground you're standing on slopes downward, you have to alter your stance, alignment, and swing.

- Stand with your shoulders and hips parallel to the slope; your right shoulder will naturally be higher than your left. You don't want to keep your shoulders level or tilt them in the opposite direction of the slope. If you do, you will likely lose your balance during the swing. You might also top the ball, because the club might bottom out early, hitting the top of the ball on the upswing.
- Position the ball more toward your back foot.
- Aim to the left of your target because balls hit off a downhill slope tend to go right.
- To help increase the ball's trajectory, use a more lofted club than you normally would for the distance.
- Expect the ball to roll farther than normal because it will fly lower from this lie. Pick a landing area short of your target to allow for the extra roll.
- Grip down on the club.
- Take approximately three-quarters of a full backswing. Feel as if you are swinging the club up the hill on the backswing and down the slope on the downswing.

Hit Off an Uphill Lie

Getting the ball into the air usually isn't a problem from an uphill lie. But because the ground you're standing on slopes upward, you need to adjust your stance, alignment, and swing.

- Stand with your shoulders and hips parallel to the upward slope; your left shoulder will naturally be higher than your right. You don't want to keep your shoulders level or tilt them in the opposite direction of the slope. If you do, you will likely lose your balance during the swing, and the club might hit the ground first, causing a fat shot.

- Position the ball toward your front foot.

- Aim to the right of your target. Balls hit off an uphill slope tend to go left because it's difficult to turn the lower body properly (gravity causes you to lean back). Your arms and hands get ahead of your body earlier than normal, which causes the clubface to close.

- Use a less lofted club than you normally would for the distance; the ball will fly higher because of the uphill slope.

- Grip down on the club.

- Feel as if you are swinging along the slope—don't hit into it. Your backswing should feel like it is going down the slope, while your downswing moves up it.

- Expect a higher trajectory and less roll. Pick a landing area close to your target.

chapter **7**

Chipping and Pitching

The majority of shots you hit during a round of golf are from 100 yards and closer to the hole. If your short game—largely made up of chipping and pitching—is not good, chances are your score will suffer the consequences. This chapter discusses how to chip and pitch the ball from the fairway and the rough and explains the stance and swing you use to execute these shots.

What Is Chipping? **90**

Chipping Stance **91**

Chipping Swing **92**

Chipping from the Fairway **93**

Chipping from the Rough **94**

What Is Pitching? **95**

Pitching Stance **96**

Pitching Swing **100**

A *chip shot* is a low, rolling shot that travels farther on the ground than it does in the air. You use this shot to advance the ball a short distance (35 yards or less) onto the green from the fairway or fringe. You can also chip from the rough if there is no bunker, water, or other hazard between you and your target. A chip shot is recommended over a pitch shot (see page XX) in these situations because it has a lower trajectory, giving you a better idea of how the ball will react when it lands. A higher trajectory means that the ball is spinning more, and it's harder to predict how the ball will land and then roll. The chipping swing also requires less motion than the pitching swing, meaning that fewer things can go wrong. So, whenever possible, go low with a chip shot.

You can use a variety of clubs to hit a chip shot, depending on the length of the shot and the placement of the pin. A 9-iron is a great club for a beginner to use because it has enough loft to get the ball into the air but still allows the ball to roll on the green. Less-lofted clubs provide even more control when you are trying to land the ball quickly and let it roll toward the target instead of landing the ball directly at or near the target. Use a less-lofted club when there is a good bit of room on the green between yourself and the hole—for example, when you are trying to chip to a hole on the opposite side of the green. A hybrid club is another good chipping option because its wider sole enables it to glide across the grass.

Chipping Stance

Unless you're standing on an uphill or downhill slope or the ball is above or below your feet, your stance should be the same for all chip shots. An *open stance* (a line drawn across the toes of both feet would point to the left of your target) helps your hips and legs clear through the swing and enables the club to come back around to your left side.

Nose in front of ball

Grip down 2 inches from end of club

Grip end ahead of clubhead

Open stance

Ball toward back foot

Weight toward front foot

TIP

Although the chipping swing is much shorter than a full swing, you still need to follow through to the finish. The clubhead might not travel more than a few feet past where the ball was, but your hips still need to rotate toward the target.

Chipping Swing

The swing for chipping is similar to a putting stroke (see Chapter 9). It's much less complicated than a full swing.

You want to keep the club low as you swing back and follow through. You never need to swing above your knees when chipping. To visualize those limits, think of a clock face: If your ball is at 6:00, then your backswing would not go past 4:00 (assuming that the clock is facing you), and your follow-through would not go past 8:00.

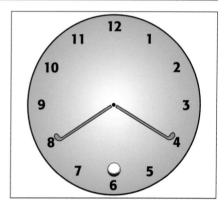

During a chip shot, your left arm and the club's shaft act as one lever-type mechanism. Always try to brush the turf after striking the ball with a descending blow. The swing itself is a miniature version of a full swing: The club travels away from the ball on a slight arc to the inside, comes back to square at impact, and then travels back to the inside after impact.

TIP

Always take a practice swing and make contact with the ground before chipping. Doing so will encourage the feeling associated with a descending blow.

If you find that you're hitting the top of the ball when chipping, move the ball a bit farther back in your stance. Doing so will help you make a descending blow down through the ball.

Chipping from the Fairway

If your approach shot lands short of the green but remains in the fairway, you can chip the ball from that spot. This shot is called a *bump and run*, where the ball lands on the ground again soon after leaving the clubface and rolls toward the target.

You have a choice of clubs when it comes to hitting a fairway chip. The longer the distance you want to cover, the lower the iron you can use. Use an 8-iron for a 30-yard or longer chip. A lower-numbered iron has less loft, which will help keep your ball lower to the ground than a higher-numbered iron with more loft.

Pitching wedge
9-iron
8-iron

As with any other chip shot, you need to determine where you want the ball to land and begin rolling toward the target. If the hole is close to the front of the green, you want to land the ball on the fairway and let it roll to the cup. If the hole is on the far side of the green, try to land the ball on the green and let it roll to the cup from there. Also keep in mind how the natural break of the green, if any, will affect your chip. Read the green, just as you would when putting (see Chapter 9). Factor in the topography—whether it slopes uphill, downhill, to the left, or to the right—when determining the appropriate landing area.

Chipping from the Rough

The type of lie you have determines the type of chip shot you make from the rough. A chip from light rough will *release*—or roll upon landing on the green—differently than one that is hit from deep rough. You use the same swing as for a greenside chip.

- If the ball is sitting up and the grass is growing in the direction of the hole, use a pitching wedge, 9-iron, or 8-iron.
- If the ball is nestled deep within the grass and the grass is growing away from the hole, use a sand wedge.
- If the ball is in heavy rough, play it more in the middle of your stance to help you get some loft, and make a more aggressive swing.

TIP

Chips hit from the rough tend to roll farther than similar shots hit from the fairway. When grass comes between the ball and the clubface, the ball does not spin as much as it would after being hit from the fairway. That makes choosing the right club and picking the best landing area very important.

A *pitch shot* is hit from close to the green and travels on a higher trajectory than a chip shot. This shot helps your ball fly over bunkers, water hazards, or rough and get close to the hole. Because you use a high-lofted club for this shot, the ball receives extra spin, giving it both height and the capability to stop quickly once it lands instead of rolling along the green as a chip shot would.

Choose a club for pitching based on your position. If you have to pitch over a bunker or water hazard to the green, use a higher-lofted club, like a pitching wedge or sand wedge (or, when your skills improve, a lob wedge, because that club has the highest degree of loft). The higher loft ensures that the ball has enough trajectory to clear the hazard and land safely on the green.

TIP

When facing a short fairway shot from just off the green that's not obstructed by hazards or rough, your first choice should be to putt. Putting will keep the ball on the ground for the entire shot, reducing the potential of a bad bounce and increasing the chance for pure impact.

Pitching Stance

Pitch shots require a wider stance than chip shots because you transfer more of your weight from back to front during the swing. You also want to grip down only 1 inch on the club and shift your weight toward your left side.

SET UP

The position of the ball in relation to your feet will change depending on the type of trajectory you want the ball to have. There are three main positions to consider, depending on whether you want to hit a low-trajectory, medium-trajectory, or high-trajectory pitch shot.

First, stand with the ball in the middle of your feet, with your heels together. Your feet should point out in opposite directions and form a V-shape. From this position, you can adjust one or both of your feet to hit a low-, medium-, or high-trajectory pitch shot. Your stance should be slightly open, with your hips and shoulders pointing just left of the target in line with your feet.

LOW-TRAJECTORY PITCH SHOT

To hit a low-trajectory pitch shot, move your left foot forward toward the target. The ball should be toward the back of your stance. The club shaft should lean forward ahead of the ball, and your hands should be positioned toward your left thigh. The follow-through on this shot remains below your waist.

CONTINUED ON NEXT PAGE

TIP

To get more roll, position the ball toward your right foot. To get more loft, play the ball toward your left foot. Think "right for roll, left for loft."

MEDIUM-TRAJECTORY PITCH SHOT

To hit a medium-trajectory pitch shot, take equal steps side to side so that the ball is in the middle of your stance. The club shaft should be in line with the ball or just slightly ahead of it, and your hands should be right in front of your zipper. Your follow-through should end waist-high.

TIP

For pitching or chipping, your left arm and the club should form a straight line, from the club shaft all the way down to the ball, at and shortly after impact, as shown here. Do not hinge your wrists.

HIGH-TRAJECTORY PITCH SHOT

To hit a high-trajectory pitch shot, move your right foot back away from the target so that the ball is forward in your stance. The club shaft should be just behind the ball, and your hands should be just to the right of your belly button. Maintain a smooth tempo throughout the swing and unhinge your wrists at impact to help add loft to the shot.

TIP

Depending on the lie you have and the club you use, the amount of roll for a pitch shot will differ by trajectory. With a sand wedge, approximate roll distances are 15 feet (high trajectory), 20 to 30 feet (medium trajectory), and more than 30 feet (low trajectory).

The players who hit the best pitch shots have a rhythmic swing, maintaining a smooth tempo on both the backswing and the downswing. A common mistake is to take a very fast downswing, which usually results in a poor shot. Maintain a steady motion, with your follow-through at least as long as your backswing.

A common pitch shot involves hitting over a greenside bunker. To execute this shot successfully, take a wide stance and relax your arms, letting them "stay long." Hinge your wrists rather than bend your left elbow, using the loft of the club to get the ball up into the air.

Take a very big backswing with a full shoulder turn, using approximately 50 percent of your energy. Hinge your wrists early in your backswing.

Throughout the swing, keep your weight toward your left foot.

TIP

Try to count the same numbers (such as 1-2-3) during your backswing and again as you swing to the finish. Doing so will help you build a smooth tempo and avoid a jerky swing.

At impact, the muscles in your wrists should feel relaxed while your hands hold the club firmly, but not tightly. Your arms should feel loose and long when you strike the ball.

As you finish the swing, the club should end up high over your left shoulder.

TIP

As a reminder to finish the swing with your hands high, imagine that you're trying not only to hit the ball over a high tree in front of you, but also that you're throwing the club over that same tree.

chapter **8**

Bunker Shots

Playing in the sand at the beach is fun. Playing in the sand on a golf course? Not so much. Unfortunately, sand bunkers are hazards you will encounter on every course. Built in all shapes and sizes, bunkers are placed along the edges (and sometimes in the middle) of fairways, as well as around greens, collecting mis-hit and misdirected shots like magnets. Unlike hitting a ball into a water hazard, though, you have a chance to get out of a bunker successfully. This chapter discusses the different types of bunkers you will encounter and how you can hit shots out of them.

Hit Out of a Greenside Bunker............104

Hit Out of a Fairway Bunker...............110

Handle Various Bunker Lies...............111

Hit Out of a Greenside Bunker

As the last line of defense for a hole, *greenside bunkers* are usually deeper and steeper than fairway bunkers, requiring you to hit a skillful shot to get the ball up over the lip and onto the putting surface. To get your ball out of a greenside bunker, you need to use the right club, maintain a good stance, enter the sand with your club at the right spot, and finish the swing properly. The club should never touch the ball throughout the swing—seriously!

USE THE RIGHT CLUB

For a greenside bunker shot, use a sand wedge or a lob wedge. These clubs need to have the proper amount of loft and "bounce" in the *sole,* or underside of the club. The leading edge of the wedge cuts through the sand, and the angle of the sole (the bounce) helps push the club back up out of the sand. Not enough bounce can cause the club to dig into the sand instead of gliding through it, resulting in fat or chunked shots that might remain in the bunker.

TIP

As a beginner, look for a sand wedge with at least 54 degrees of loft and more than 10 degrees of bounce. As your bunker skills improve, you might want to purchase a wedge with 60 degrees of loft and 8 degrees of bounce. The degree of bounce is often indicated on a wedge. If it isn't, ask the salesperson for that information or consult a PGA/LPGA professional.

ADJUST YOUR STANCE

For stability purposes, your greenside bunker stance should be slightly wider than for a normal fairway shot, with your knees flexed a bit more. Position the ball between your belt buckle and your front foot. Dig your feet into the sand to help maintain your balance. Doing so is especially important if your ball is on an uphill or downhill lie.

Most of your weight should be on your front foot. Open the clubface slightly to let the bounce of the club do its job.

Your stance should be open *slightly* to the target line. If your stance is too open, the club will skim the sand and glance across the ball, resulting in a line drive that sails past the hole or even over the green.

TIP

Always enter a bunker at its lowest point. Never jump into a bunker. Doing so can damage the bunker, not to mention your own body.

CONTINUED ON NEXT PAGE

BACKSWING

The greenside bunker swing is very similar to a standard swing from the fairway (see Chapter 3), with your wrists hinged earlier in the backswing. Because you will likely be facing a short shot, your backswing doesn't need to go too far back. For a longer greenside bunker shot, however, the length of your backswing should increase accordingly, and your stance and clubface should be less open.

TIP

In the photo above on the right, notice how the left arm is parallel to the ground and forms a 90-degree angle with the club shaft. This indicates a comfortable wrist hinge that will encourage the clubhead speed necessary to execute this shot successfully.

IMPACT

At impact, your hands should be even with or slightly behind the clubhead. The club should hit the sand first, approximately 1 to 2 inches behind the ball. As the club slides through the sand, you should hear a thump, and the ball should come out high and land softly. If your swing is too steep, the club will dig too deep into the sand and not propel the ball upward—leaving you with another sand shot.

Accelerate through the shot; do not slow down as your club enters the sand. You are trying to splash sand out of the bunker; if you don't do that, the ball won't move.

TIP

The quality of sand used in bunkers differs from course to course, so the point at which your club should enter the sand will vary slightly. If the sand is very fluffy, you want to enter it a bit farther behind the ball than you would if the sand were wet and compact.

CONTINUED ON NEXT PAGE

Your club should not touch the ball at any time during a greenside bunker shot. You should aim for a spot approximately 1 inch behind the ball. The wedge will cut through the sand underneath the ball, lifting it up into the air without actually making contact with it.

Although you need to swing the clubhead through the sand on this shot, remember that your club cannot touch the sand or the ball *prior to* your swing. This is known as *grounding your club.* If you do so while in a bunker, you will incur a penalty stroke.

FOLLOW THROUGH

A good follow-through is essential to a successful bunker shot. Stopping at impact will affect the distance and height of the shot. Completing the swing with your hands and club high in the air should result in a more powerful swing and generate the force you need to advance the ball out of the bunker.

A proper finish means staying in balance with your weight over your front foot. You should not be leaning backward at the finish unless you are hitting from an uphill lie.

Hit Out of a Fairway Bunker

Fairway bunkers are longer and shallower than greenside bunkers and are usually found on one or both sides of a fairway. Course designers frequently place a bunker at the corner of a *dogleg hole* (a hole that bends to the right or left) to foil players' attempts to take the shortest path to the pin. Bunkers are sometimes placed in the middle of fairways as well. Keep in mind a few major differences between a greenside bunker shot and a fairway bunker shot.

In a fairway bunker:

- You hit the ball first, not the sand first. You are trying to pick the ball cleanly off the sand and leave a divot *in front of* where your ball was positioned, not behind it or directly under it.

- You stand tall with your feet dug into the sand only slightly for balance. Your legs do less work than in a greenside bunker; you want to keep your lower body as still as possible. Consequently, you must take at least one more club than you would normally use. For example, if you would ordinarily hit a 7-iron from that distance, use a 6-iron to hit out of the bunker.

- You take a longer, fuller swing than in a greenside bunker.

- You might not be able to reach the green. Study the hole and plan your fairway bunker shot based on where you want to play your next shot from.

Handle Various Bunker Lies

The type of lie you have in a bunker determines how your ball will react after you complete the swing.

STANDARD

Sitting on top of the sand—almost as if the ball is teed up—is the best possible position for the ball to be in. It provides an excellent chance for you to slide your wedge through the sand underneath the ball. From this lie, the ball will *check,* or quickly stop rolling on the green, due to spin. Make sure that your target landing area is fairly close to the cup.

BURIED

A high shot that lands directly in a bunker, especially one filled with very soft sand, can end up "buried," or as a "fried egg" (because that's what it looks like). This type of lie requires a more closed clubface to offset the amount of sand around the ball. You can expect the ball to come out low with lots of roll from this lie, so make sure to pick a landing area well short of your target.

CONTINUED ON NEXT PAGE

UPHILL

If your ball sits on an uphill slope in a bunker, you need to adjust your stance accordingly. The tendency is to lean into the sand and keep your shoulders perpendicular to the horizon, but doing so will cause the club to dig into the sand and the ball to go nowhere.

Wrong

Instead, your shoulders should tilt in the direction of the bunker's slope, both in your stance and throughout your swing. Your weight is mostly on your back foot, but not so much that you lose your balance. The ball will land softly on the green without much roll because of the shot's higher trajectory, so make sure to pick a landing area very close to your target.

Correct

DOWNHILL

If your ball rests on a downhill slope in a bunker, you need to adjust your stance accordingly. The tendency is to lean into the sand and keep your shoulders perpendicular to the horizon.

Wrong

Instead, your shoulders should tilt downward in the direction of the bunker's slope, both in your stance and throughout your swing. Your weight is mostly on your front foot, but not so much that you lose your balance. This shot will have a lower trajectory and therefore more roll when it lands on the green, so pick a landing area well short of your target. To offset the lower trajectory, open the clubface and aim your feet slightly left of the target.

Correct

chapter 9

Putting

Getting the ball into the hole in as few strokes as possible is the ultimate goal of golf. The final step in that process comes on the green, where the art of putting comes into play. Putts make up almost half of your score during every round.

Every putting surface is different, but having a basic understanding of how to read greens and putt with a smooth stroke will improve your score dramatically. This chapter discusses how you grip the putter, the proper putting stance and swing, and specific goals for different types of putts.

Putting Routine 116

Grip the Putter 119

Take Your Stance 121

Make the Swing 125

Read the Green 127

Control the Distance 129

Rushing to hit a 2-foot putt or not focusing properly on a 40-footer often results in misses or uncomfortably long second putts. Developing a consistent putting routine will help you focus on the putt no matter what the distance. Here is the putting routine we recommend:

1 Mark the position of your ball on the green by placing a flat object (such as a coin) directly behind and as close as possible to the ball. Return the ball as close as possible to the original spot.

2 Study the putt you're facing. Get low to the ground to read the green and see how the ground is shaped. Use that information to choose an intermediate target spot for your putt. If the green is flat, your intermediate target spot will be along the line to the hole. If the green slopes to the left or right, your target will be a point along that break where the ball will start to turn toward the hole.

TIP

If other players putt before you, watch their putts to see how they move. Keep in mind that proper etiquette dictates that you never stand directly on another golfer's putting line, which extends from behind the golfer to beyond the hole.

3 When it's your turn to putt, replace your ball and pick up your marker.

4 Stand behind or beside the ball and take a practice swing.

5 Place the putter behind the ball and then take your stance.

CONTINUED ON NEXT PAGE

TIP

To help you line up the ball properly, point the ball's brand name in the direction you are hitting. You can also draw a line around the ball to help you with alignment. Doing so also enables you to learn whether you struck the ball in the middle of the clubface. If the ball rolls with the line spinning end over end straight toward the target, then you hit it solidly in the right spot. If the line wobbles to one side or the other, then you struck the ball off-center.

6 Look at your target spot again.

7 Make your stroke and follow through.

TIP

After getting into position over the ball, just prior to making your stroke, exhale. Doing so relaxes your muscles and relieves tension— one of the primary reasons for missing putts.

The grip you use to hold a putter is entirely your choice. Potential grip styles include standard, cross-handed, and the Claw, but none will be effective for you unless you're comfortable using it. Experiment with each of the grips described below on the practice green to see which one works best.

STANDARD

1 Hang your arms naturally in front of your body so that your palms are open flat and facing each other. Bend forward slightly at the waist so that your eyes are directly over the ball.

2 Place the putter between your facing palms.

3 Grasp the putter with both hands. Your thumbs should rest on the front of the putter grip.

4 Exert equal (but light) pressure with both hands on the grip throughout the putting stroke.

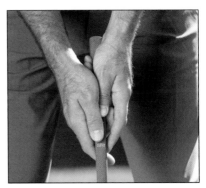

TIP

With this grip, both hands work together as one unit. If your hands are apart from each other, then returning the putter to a square position at impact with the ball is much more difficult.

CONTINUED ON NEXT PAGE

CROSS-HANDED

The cross-handed grip is the same as the standard grip except that you reverse the positions of your hands: Your left hand is below your right hand (the opposite for lefties). This grip forces you to keep your shoulders more level with the green and helps prevent your wrists from hinging.

CLAW

"The Claw" is a last resort for players who are not comfortable or successful with other grips. It is designed to help combat the uncertainty of the hand motion during the putting stroke and is one step away from swinging the putter one-handed. The position of the right hand prevents any hinging motion in the right wrist. The top (or left) hand holds the club as in the standard grip, but the club is tucked between the thumb and palm of the lower (right) hand. The right hand remains open and pointing toward the ground in front of the club.

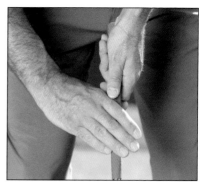

TIP

While trying to establish the grip you are most comfortable with, play a few complete rounds using a particular style. Doing so gives you a reasonable chance to develop an authentic feel on the greens. Frequently changing grips, especially during a single round, will only lead to more indecision when it comes time to make an important putt.

As with your grip, your putting stance should be whatever is most comfortable for you. However, there are elements of a good, basic putting stance that you should adopt.

1 Before taking your stance, stand next to or behind the ball, look at the target, and take a practice swing that mirrors the length and tempo required for the putt. Looking at the hole instead of the ball can help you get a feel for the stroke and visualize the path you want the ball to follow.

2 Place the putter directly behind the ball, aiming at your target. Your arms should hang relaxed and close to your body, with a little bend in the elbows. Notice how the shaft of the putter and the right forearm are in line.

CONTINUED ON NEXT PAGE

3 Once your putter is in position behind the ball, step in first with your right foot and then with your left foot.

Because your ball and your putter are facing directly at the intended path of your putt, your feet and shoulders should be square to that line. Your eyes are directly over the ball.

4 After taking your stance, make sure that the ball is positioned just forward of center between your feet. Your feet should be no wider than shoulder-width apart—slightly less than that is ideal. This setup enables you to strike the ball with a level or slightly ascending blow, which helps it roll forward consistently. It also reduces the likelihood of the ball taking any hops or bounces.

5 Make sure that the putter is lying level on the ground when you place it behind the ball. You have the best chance to aim properly and hit the ball solidly with the putter flat on the ground. If the toe of the putter (the end farther away from you) is up in the air, the upright lie angle will cause you to aim left. If the heel of the putter (the end closer to you) is up in the air, the flat lie angle will cause you to aim right.

6 Make sure that the ball is positioned in the middle of the clubface. Because the mass of the putter is usually located in the center of the clubface, hitting the ball off to either side of center will decrease both the amount of power at impact and accuracy.

TIP

If your eyes are over the ball and the heel or toe end of the putter is still up in the air, your putter may not fit you correctly. In that case, talk to a PGA or LPGA professional regarding the length and lie angle of your putter and find out whether you should switch to a different putter.

CONTINUED ON NEXT PAGE

Putting **123**

In a good putting stance, your weight is balanced between both feet or slightly favors the left side. Your arms hang naturally in front of you and your hands are in line with the ball.

You do not want to stand with your hands too far behind the ball, or your wrists will be bent at impact. Bent wrists add loft to the putter and cause the ball to bounce or hop after being struck.

The putting stroke is shorter and simpler than the other swings you use on the course, but you must do several important things.

After you get into your stance, but before you take your swing, look one more time at your target line and exhale. Picture your hands and shoulders moving together as one unit.

During the backswing, your head should be steady and your weight should remain as it was at address.

At impact, your hands, your shoulders, and the putter form a triangle, as shown. Keep this position intact throughout the stroke.

TIP

During the backswing, allow the putter to swing slightly to the inside before coming back to square at impact and finishing slightly inside on the follow-through. As you turn your body to bring the putter back, this swing path should happen naturally.

CONTINUED ON NEXT PAGE

Bending your wrists at impact will affect the speed and direction of your putt. If you find yourself doing so, then you have taken too long of a backswing, and you will have difficulty controlling speed and accuracy. Your wrists and shoulders should move together, remaining in the triangle position.

Follow through after impact, with the putter passing by your left leg or farther depending on the distance of the putt. The length of your backswing should equal the length of your follow-through. For example, if your putter goes back to the pinky toe of your right foot, then it should go forward to the pinky toe of your left foot.

TIP

The amount of backswing you should take depends on the distance of your putt; the longer the putt, the longer the backswing you should use.

Most greens are made up of multiple sections with slopes that can cause a ball to move right, left, downhill, and/or uphill. That makes *reading the green*—or predicting which way the ball will move after being hit—especially important.

A straight line (represented by the string extended from the putter to the hole in the second photo on this page) might be the shortest path to the hole on a level green, but topography often forces the ball to travel along a curved path. This curve is called *break*.

A putt usually breaks left or right to some degree. The break could be dramatic, forcing a wide, curving putt, as shown here, or subtle, where the ball curves just slightly. Some putts involve a double break, where the ball moves in one direction and then the other.

CONTINUED ON NEXT PAGE

Reading a green starts from the fairway. Study your surroundings as you walk toward the green, because greens often slope in certain directions, such as away from a nearby mountain (a high spot) or toward a body of water (a low spot). Look at the ground the green sits on; you can even study the angle of the cup to get an idea of how the green's surface might slope. Then proceed to the green itself.

The best way to read a green is to look at the putting surface from behind your ball. Make sure your eyes are parallel to the horizon. Crouching down close to the ground will help you see whether the surface is level or tilted in a certain direction. If time and pace of play allow, you can also look at the green from the other direction, with the hole between you and the ball. Walking alongside the area between your ball and the hole is another good way to judge the green's slope. You should also "go to school" on putts hit by other players—see how their balls react to the putting surface and learn what impact those reactions might have on your putt.

The ultimate goal of every putt is to get the ball into the hole. The length of the putt and whether it will travel uphill or downhill affect the amount of power you should put behind your stroke. It's also a matter of *lag putting*—getting the putt at least close to the hole so that you're left with a much shorter and more makeable second (and hopefully final) putt.

LONG PUTTS

For long putts, distance is more important than accuracy. Imagine a 3-foot circle around the hole—you are aiming at the hole but trying to put enough pace on the ball so that if it doesn't go in, it will come to rest inside that circle, leaving you with a makeable second putt.

An alternate image for long putts is a 3-foot circle directly *behind* the hole. This image can help ensure that your putt reaches the hole or finishes past it, giving you a better chance of making it. A putt that doesn't reach the hole has zero chance of going in.

CONTINUED ON NEXT PAGE

UPHILL PUTTS

On uphill putts, pick a point past the hole as your target. Doing so will ensure that you hit the ball firmly enough that it will go up the hill and ideally stop in or near the hole, as opposed to stopping short of the hole or even rolling back down the hill.

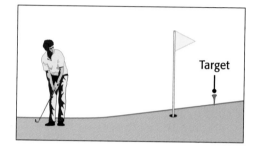

DOWNHILL PUTTS

On downhill putts, pick a spot in front of the hole as your target, as indicated by the tee in the illustration. Doing so enables the natural slope of the green to carry the ball the rest of the way without it going too far past the hole if it doesn't go in.

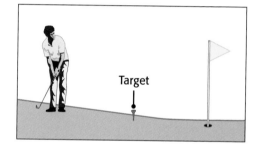

TIP

If your ball is up against the *collar* (where the fairway or greenside rough meets the fringe of the green), or the fringe grass is especially long, see "Putting from the Fringe" on the next page to play the shot with a putter, or consider these options:

- Use a wedge and hit the ball with the bottom edge (called *blading*) to avoid getting caught in the grass.
- Use a hybrid, 5-wood, or 7-wood—the larger clubhead will move through the grass more easily than a putter. Choke down on the club, keep the ball in the center of your stance, and stand closer to the ball than you normally would.

PUTTING FROM THE FRINGE

Putting from the *fringe*—the closely mown turf immediately surrounding the putting surface—is an added challenge when it comes to distance control. Because fringe grass is slightly higher than the actual putting surface, you need to strike the ball firmly in order to move it onto the green. The fringe grass will take speed off the putt immediately, so you must increase the length of your backswing accordingly.

PUTTING FROM THE FAIRWAY

Some holes have an open entrance to the green, without high grass, water hazards, or bunkers preventing you from putting directly from the fairway toward the hole. Check the condition of the grass in this area to judge the pace needed to get the ball onto the green and close to the hole. The higher the grass, the more speed is needed. If there is a sprinkler head in your line, or if the condition of the grass is inconsistent, then it's better to chip the ball (see Chapter 7).

10

Troubleshooting

So much of your body is involved in the golf swing—your hands, your arms, your legs, your shoulders, and of course your brain—that, for beginners, hitting the ball straight can be considered a small miracle. Your odds of repeating that result will improve as you gain experience, but things will go wrong, largely because the path that your club follows during the swing is off.

Hitting slice after slice or repeatedly popping the ball up into the air gets frustrating quickly. With the proper techniques, however, you can solve these problems. This chapter tackles troublesome shots on the course and gives you some drills that will help prevent your swing from going wrong in the first place.

Fix a Slice **134**

Fix a Hook. **139**

Avoid Hitting Fat Shots **142**

Avoid Hitting Thin or Topping. **144**

Stop Hitting Pop-Ups. **146**

Stop Hitting Line Drives **147**

Most golfers play right-handed, and most of them slice the ball. *Slice* is the name for a shot that curves dramatically from left to right (not to be confused with a *fade*, which also curves from left to right, but on purpose and in a controlled manner; or a *push*, where the ball moves directly to the right immediately after being hit).

WHAT CAUSES A SLICE

A slice is caused by an open clubface coming across the ball—glancing against it instead of striking it squarely. You might have been aiming straight at the target (represented by the bottom board in the photo), but the club is coming down across the ball and heading too far to the left of the target, as represented by the top board in the photo.

FAQ

Can I use a slice to my advantage?

Only in very limited situations is a slice useful. For instance, if you're hitting to a fairway that bends severely to the right, a slice can curve around that bend. In virtually every other situation, though, a slice will do you more harm than good. Better to work on fixing it than to try working around it!

SHOULDERS DRILL

A major problem that causes slicing is allowing your shoulders to turn too quickly through the downswing, which can make it difficult to square the clubface at impact. To slow them down, try this drill.

Lay a board (or a club) down on the ground pointing toward a target. Assume your stance in front of the board and extend your left arm to hold the top of your driver, which should rest on the other side of the board. Hold a second club in your right hand, as if to hit a ball.

Slowly swing the club in your right hand through the opening between your body and the board on the ground while keeping your left hand on top of the driver in front of you. This drill helps slow the rotation of your shoulders during the swing, which promotes a square clubface at impact and reduces the likelihood of a swing that comes across the ball.

CONTINUED ON NEXT PAGE

HANDS DRILL

If your hands are not in the proper position during the swing, the chances of your clubface being square at impact are slim—and that's when a slice can happen. Here's a drill you can do to get a feel for the correct position of your left hand.

Hold a ball in your left hand while your right hand rests on top of a club. Move your left hand through a regular swing motion while holding onto the ball.

As you take your left hand through the swing motion, you should see half of the ball facing up at the point of impact. When you get to the follow-through position (your left palm should be facing up), you should see the entire ball, because your hands will have rolled over during the swing. This drill helps you release (or roll over) your hands through the swing, enabling you to square the clubface and providing more power when you strike the ball. If you don't release your hands, the clubhead won't turn over properly, and you might find yourself slicing the ball.

Next, put a club in your hand and make a partial swing. Try to re-create the feeling and motion you experienced when the ball was in your left hand.

Note: The position of the clubhead in the photo is exaggerated to emphasize the left hand position. Ideally, the toe of the club would be pointing up in the air.

Do this drill as often as possible on the course, including while you wait for other players to tee off or while awaiting your turn on the fairway.

CONTINUED ON NEXT PAGE

MISS THE BUCKET DRILL

If you're slicing shots to the right or pulling shots to the left, you are swinging the club too far outside to inside on the downswing. If the club continues on this path, you will pull the ball to the left. If you try to adjust the position of the club with your hands, you will open the clubface and cut across the ball, leading to a slice.

The buckets you see on driving ranges can do more than just hold range balls. You can use one to work on building the proper swing path. Place a bucket (ideally an empty one) just ahead of your front foot, between yourself and the ball. Take a swing and try to avoid hitting the bucket. Doing so encourages you to swing from inside to square to outside—an exaggeration of the proper inside-square-inside swing path (see "Swing Path" in Chapter 5), but useful to help correct the outside-to-inside path that causes a slice.

A *hook* is the opposite of a slice—and equally undesirable. A hooked ball curves dramatically from right to left (not to be confused with a *draw*, which also moves from right to left, but on purpose and in a controlled manner; or a *pull*, where the ball moves directly to the left immediately after being struck).

WHAT CAUSES A HOOK

A hooked shot happens either when the clubhead gets ahead of your hands at impact, causing the clubface to hit the ball in a closed position, or the swing path of the club is excessively inside to outside. Remember, your goal is for the club to travel on an inside-to-square-to-inside swing path.

TIP

Hooked shots can also be caused by a grip that is too strong in either hand. A strong grip promotes a closed clubface (useful for hitting a draw, but also the cause of a hook). In this situation, a more neutral grip will help you square the clubface and likely reduce the number of hooked shots you hit.

CONTINUED ON NEXT PAGE

MISS THE BUCKET DRILL

If you're pushing the ball to the right or hooking shots to the left, you are probably swinging on an inside-to-outside path instead of an inside-to-square-to-inside path. If the clubface stays square to that path, you will hit a push shot. If you try to adjust the position of the club with your hands, you will likely turn the clubhead over at impact and hook the ball left.

To work on correcting your swing path, grab a bucket from the driving range. Place the bucket (either empty or full of practice balls) just behind your back foot and between yourself and the ball.

Then take a swing, making sure that your club misses the bucket on the downswing. During the downswing, keep the club in front of the bucket. This motion exaggerates what a proper swing should feel like, but doing so will help you correct the problem. You want to feel your hips open up to the target, with your hands and the clubhead following to the left (or inside) after you hit the ball. When you reach the finish position, the bottom of your back foot should be turned up and facing the bucket.

IMPACT DRILL

In an ideal swing, the clubhead compresses squarely against the back of the ball at impact. To make this happen, the club shaft must lean slightly forward so that your hands line up with the ball before the clubhead gets to the same position.

To practice the feeling of a square clubface at impact, place the end of a two-by-four where the ball would normally be. Set up with the clubhead touching the end of the board. Then assume the impact position: Your hips should be starting to open up toward the target, your hands ahead of the clubhead, your left wrist flat.

Slowly push the board toward the target. Repeat a few times; then replace the board with a ball and hit some half-shots. Doing so will help you break the habit of getting the clubhead ahead of your hands, which results in hooked shots.

If your hands are behind the clubhead at impact, the clubhead will start to rise up the board instead of feeling like it is going down into the ground. This can result in a closed clubface—and a hook. You will also feel your weight hanging back on your right side instead of having moved to your left side. If a ball were there, you might hit the upper half (known as "topping" the shot).

Hitting the ball *fat* means that the clubhead hits the ground before making contact with the ball, resulting in a big divot and much less distance than you expected. This problem is caused by swinging the club on an inside-to-outside path and failing to hit the ball squarely, or a poor weight transfer from your back foot to your front foot.

CORRECT YOUR WEIGHT SHIFT DRILL

A proper weight shift will help prevent not only fat shots, but also weak slices and dramatic hooks. Many golfers allow their weight to move to the outside of the right foot during the backswing, making it more difficult to shift it forward during the downswing. The end result is an off-balance swing, because the weight never moves to the front foot.

To practice your weight shift, place a ball underneath the outside of your back foot and take a normal swing, making sure not to lose your balance. If your back foot starts to wobble, apply more pressure to the inside of that foot.

This drill encourages you to keep your weight in the correct place during the backswing and the downswing, causing you to finish properly with your weight on your front leg.

TIP

An overactive lower body during a swing means that your legs drive laterally toward the target during the downswing, with both knees staying flexed. This lateral leg drive keeps the club traveling down the target line too long after impact rather than coming back around to the inside. Focus on straightening your left leg at impact, with your weight going into your left heel. This will help your hips open up faster and enable the club to swing back to the inside after the ball is hit.

Avoid Hitting Thin or Topping

Tense arms that pull in toward your body at impact, along with a far too active lower body (moving your weight forward too quickly or changing your posture during the swing), can lead to thin or topped shots. Either action positions the club just high enough that it hits the middle (thin) or top (topped) of the ball, resulting in a line drive (thin) that can't be controlled or a ball that hits the ground immediately rather than going up into the air (topped). These drills will help you fix these problems.

FEET TOGETHER DRILL

To avoid hitting thin or topping, try taking half-swings with your feet together. Doing so will help you learn how to swing your arms and the clubhead freely back to the ball without your lower body interfering. Try to keep your arms relaxed during the half-swing so that they can remain extended through impact.

Place a tee in the ground where your ball would normally be. Put a second tee an inch or two in front of the other, with both lined up in the direction of a target.

Stand with your feet together and take a half-swing to feel the sensation of the clubhead turning over while your lower body stays quiet. Doing so will slow down your hip rotation during the swing and help you reach a square clubhead position at impact.

Keeping your feet together makes it harder for your hips to open toward the target too soon, and makes it harder for your shoulders to rotate too quickly. Hitting both tees also improves your ability to take a proper divot by hitting down and through where the ball would be.

Practice this drill in three phases:

- First, try to clip both tees out of the ground to get "longer" at impact.

- Then pick a spot on the ground and practice hitting it. Try to create a divot in front of the spot, not behind it.

- Finally, put a ball down and try to hit the ball first and then the ground. Pretend that there is a tee under the ball, and swing as if you were trying to hit the imaginary tee.

You might hear other golfers use the phrase "hit it thin to win." This phrase refers to the rare situation in which a thin shot actually finishes near the intended target. That result is almost always a fluke; you want to eliminate thin or topped shots from your game as much as possible.

If your shots are popping straight up into the air, your club is approaching the ball at too steep an angle and with a face that is too open. You are likely taking the club up into the air and then straight down to the ball at a steep angle, as shown here. The solution is to create a flatter, more sweeping arc and a square clubface at impact—think of a U-shaped swing rather than a V-shaped swing.

HIGH TEE DRILL

To promote a flatter swing and solid contact, especially with long irons and hybrids, tee a ball up as high as you can. Only a flatter swing will be able to make solid contact with a ball in this position; if your swing is still too steep, you will hit the tee, and the ball will go straight up into the air. You will also be reminded of the importance of squaring the clubface through impact. If the ball flies high and right, then your clubface is still open.

Stop Hitting Line Drives

If your shots are staying low to the ground and not going in the direction you're aiming (known as *line drives* or *skulled shots*), the club's leading edge—the very bottom of the clubface—is hitting the middle of the ball. Sliding your head past the ball prior to impact can cause this problem. If you slide your head, your upper body is beating your lower body to the ball.

Want a visual image to remind you to remain steady and keep your head behind the ball? Imagine an iron a few inches from the side of your head. You wouldn't want your head to make contact with a hot iron, would you?

TIP

Here's another drill to try. Put a second ball an inch or two behind the ball you want to hit and place your club between the two balls. As you start your backswing, try to push the second ball backward with the clubhead. Doing so helps prevent an early wrist cock and decreases any potential chopping motion in your swing, thereby creating a flatter, U-shaped swing.

chapter 11

Drills

There's no way around it—you have to practice to get better at golf. That does not mean hitting countless buckets of balls on the range day after day, however; instead, focus on specific drills that will help you develop the variety of shots you will need to play well. To complement drills and tips given in earlier chapters, this chapter reviews numerous additional drills to address many of the shots you will face out on the course.

Driver Drills **150**

Iron Drills **154**

Chipping/Pitching Drills **159**

Bunker Drills **163**

Putting Drills **166**

Driving is the ultimate combination of power and accuracy. Staying in control and in balance during the swing is an important key to finding the fairway. These drills will help you achieve that goal.

HEAR THE SWOOSH

To ensure that your driver (or any other club's) swing reaches its fastest point at the very bottom of the swing, listen for the swoosh sound. Instead of holding the club at the grip end, hold it toward the clubhead end. Then make a swing without hitting a ball or allowing the club to touch the ground. Ideally, you should hear the sound just as the club passes where the ball would normally be on the ground.

If you hear a swoosh early in the backswing, you are releasing the energy behind the swing too early and losing the proper angle. This usually results in an over-the-top swing that can produce a slice or hook.

No sound

Swoosh

THE SHADOW KNOWS

Because the driver is the longest club you will use for a tee shot, the chance of getting your head in front of the ball prior to impact is greater. It's very important to keep your head behind the ball, even slightly after impact. To make sure that your head stays in the proper position, try this drill:

1. Stand in a spot where your body casts a shadow out in front of you.
2. Address the ball as if you were going to make a swing. Look at your shadow to make sure that your head is behind the ball.
3. Take some practice swings. While doing so, look at your shadow again to make sure that your head remains behind the ball until slightly after impact. (It's okay for your head to move forward at the completion of the swing.)

CONTINUED ON NEXT PAGE

HIGH TEE

Pulling, slicing, or popping up shots is often the result of swinging the driver at too steep an angle. To help fix that problem, tee a ball as high up as possible. Then take a swing and try to hit only the ball and not the tee. Doing so successfully means that you have made a sweeping stroke rather than a steep one.

IN-N-OUT

To help correct an outside-to-inside swing path that can generate a sharp slice or hook, place two tees in the ground: one where your ball would normally go when hitting a driver (off the inside of your left heel) and the other 2 inches to the right and 2 inches below the first tee. At first, do not place a ball on either tee; simply make your swing and try to clip both tees on your downswing. Doing so helps create the proper inside-to-outside swing path.

FIRST BASE

Another swing path image to keep in mind while practicing with your driver is this: Picture your ball teed up at home plate on a baseball diamond. Visualize where first base would be located and swing the club in that direction to achieve an inside-to-outside path on the downswing.

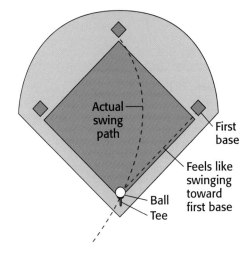

Actual swing path

First base

Feels like swinging toward first base

Ball

Tee

LOW CEILING

The longer the club, the flatter the swing you should make. The swing you make with a driver is not the same swing you use with an 8-iron. As you take your stance with the driver, imagine that you are standing in a room with a low ceiling. During your swing, you do not want to make contact with the ceiling.

A consistent swing is important for every club in your bag, but especially so with irons, because these clubs are the ones that most often get the ball onto the green. The drills in this section cover the posture, weight transfer, and arm extension you need to maintain throughout the iron swing.

LEARN FROM YOUR DIVOTS

Your divots are valuable learning tools that can help you eliminate fat shots. To create a proper divot, you need to hit the ball first and then the turf.

To see whether you're hitting the ground in the proper position, draw a line perpendicular to your target and place a ball on the line, or put a tee just beyond the ball. After hitting the ball, take a look at the divot you created. The divot should be *in front of* that line or tee, as shown here. (The ball in the photo is just below where it would have been prior to being hit.) If the divot starts behind the line or tee, then you're hitting the ground before hitting the ball—not good.

The width of your divot says a lot, too. It should be as wide as the face of the club you used. A narrower divot indicates that your clubface was not square to the target at impact.

DIVOT DIRECTIONS

For this drill, lay a board on the ground, pointing toward your target. Place a ball between yourself and the board and take a swing.

If your divot is pointing right, toward the target line (indicated by the white board), you have likely pushed the ball to the right.

If your divot is pointing left, away from the target line, you have likely pulled or sliced your shot.

TIP

In either situation, your swing isn't necessarily the problem, especially if you don't have a board to guide you. Your stance might have been pointing to the right or left of the target when you set up for the shot, eliminating any chance you had of hitting the ball where you wanted to. Know your target line so that you can check your divot in relation to how you set up for the shot.

CONTINUED ON NEXT PAGE

FULL EXTENSION

Not hitting crisp iron shots? Then you're scooping at the ball instead of hitting down on it. One cause of that problem is your right elbow being too far from your body during the swing. To correct that, practice short chip shots. When the club hits the ball, your left arm should be fully extended and your right elbow should be close to your body. You don't have to take a full swing—in fact, you can stop right after impact. At that point, good iron players have their hands just past their body and the clubhead a little right of the hands. Having the clubhead left of the hands produces more of a flipping motion.

POSTURE

Keeping your spine in the proper position throughout the swing gives you a better chance of hitting the ball squarely at impact. Pulling your body away from the ball usually affects your swing path negatively and can lead to slices and/or hooks.

To practice maintaining your spine angle, make sure that your left shoulder is lower than your right shoulder at the top of the backswing.

During your follow-through, your right shoulder should be lower than your left shoulder.

CONTINUED ON NEXT PAGE

WEIGHT TRANSFER

To get the feel of shifting your weight forward during the swing, try this drill. Start with your feet together and make a full turn to the top of the backswing. Then step toward your target with your left foot and swing to the finish. You initiate the forward movement with that step to encourage a positive weight transfer, not unlike stepping into a baseball pitch or hitting a forehand in tennis.

WHERE'S YOUR LEFT ELBOW?

Having a one-piece takeaway (or backswing) helps you create more power and a better swing path. As you start your backswing, keep your left elbow against your stomach. This drill gets your shoulders moving to the right as opposed to just the club or your arms moving back.

Chipping/ Pitching Drills

Both chip shots and pitch shots require a tremendous amount of touch to get the ball close to the target. Practice these types of shots to reduce the number of strokes you take near the green—a sure way to improve your overall score. This section contains some practice drills that will help you improve your chipping and pitching skills.

UNBREAKABLE

To practice an important part of chipping—not breaking your wrists at impact—take two clubs together in your hands, holding one in the regular position on the grip and the other on the shaft close to the clubhead, as shown.

The second club keeps your wrists out of the shot and enables your left arm and the club to act as one. If you break your wrists at impact, you will feel the shaft of the second club hit your rib cage at impact. In a proper swing, that club will never make contact with your body.

TIP

If you find yourself breaking your wrists too much, you might be trying too hard to get the ball into the air. Instead, let the club's loft do the work.

CONTINUED ON NEXT PAGE

MISS THE TEES

When chipping or pitching, you want to make a descending blow at impact. For this drill, place two tees next to each other 2 inches behind the ball. Practice hitting down on the ball by avoiding contact with the two tees.

If you swing incorrectly, your club will hit one or both of the tees prior to hitting the ball, and you will likely top the ball and hit a line drive that sails far past your target.

ONE-ARM SWINGS

To develop a feel for the ball on the club-face, try hitting short chip shots with the ball teed up and only your left hand on the club. Your left arm stays straight through the swing, and the shaft should lean forward at the start (hand ahead of the ball) and at impact to ensure that you hit down on the ball. Think of it as a quiet stroke because your lower body is not moving much, if at all.

For pitch shots, try hitting with only your right hand on the club. Do not hinge your right wrist as you come into the ball. Instead, focus on rotating your hips to the left as you hit through the ball.

CONTINUED ON NEXT PAGE

HANDS AHEAD

To help keep your hands ahead of the clubhead while chipping, try keeping the butt end of the club against your left arm during your setup. Rest it there against the inside of your forearm during the stroke instead of hinging and unhinging your wrists. Doing so provides more consistent power; doing otherwise leaves more room for error and can lead to skulled and fat shots, plus it makes it harder to predict the distance of your shot.

MISS THE BACK BALL

If the Miss the Tees drill (see page 160) is not working, try this similar drill. Place a ball approximately 6 inches behind the ball you will hit. Avoid hitting the second ball during your backswing and downswing to help create a descending blow.

Bunker Drills

Few shots are more frustrating than a shot from a bunker that doesn't leave the bunker on the first attempt. While your overall goal is to avoid these situations, the following drills will help build the confidence and skills you'll need to escape the sand efficiently.

HIT THE LINE

The point at which the club enters the sand on a greenside bunker shot heavily influences the outcome. Draw two lines in the sand an inch or two apart. Try to hit the first line with your club, and make sure that your divot carries to the second line, where your ball would normally be positioned. If you hit too far in front of the first line or hit the second line first, you will not execute a proper greenside bunker shot. Hitting the first line ensures that your club will go just underneath the ball and get it airborne.

SPLASH AROUND

During a successful greenside bunker shot, the sand will splash forward after being hit by your club. Without using a ball, swing your wedge in a bunker and practice that sensation of splashing the sand out of the bunker. Be sure to rake the bunker after you're done!

CONTINUED ON NEXT PAGE

STAND ON GLASS

During a fairway bunker shot, you want to keep your lower body as still (or "quiet") as possible. Imagine that you are standing on a piece of glass. You don't want to break the glass during the swing. Instead, you want to hit the ball first, and not the sand, without a lot of movement in your legs or feet.

TEE IT UP

For a greenside bunker shot, you want to hit the sand first. Try teeing a ball up in the bunker so that the ball is slightly above the sand. Then take a swing, aiming to hit the tee out of the sand.

BUNKER BALANCE

To eliminate the tendency to fall back to the right in an attempt to help the ball up into the air, try hitting a bunker shot standing mainly on your left leg. (Keep your right big toe touching the ground to maintain your balance.) Remember to aim 1 to 2 inches behind the ball, keep your head steady, and swing the club through the sand.

A DOLLAR'S WORTH

To visualize the correct entry and exit point of the club during a bunker shot, imagine a dollar bill placed flat under the ball. That's the length of the sand divot you want to take. If it's longer, you will likely hit a fat shot that does not move the ball forward much. If it's shorter, you may hit the ball first instead of the sand.

The best part about practicing your putting is that you don't need a driving range. You can use virtually any surface (your living room carpet, a hallway, and so on) and substitute a cup for the hole to roll some putts and practice your routine. The ideal venue is a practice green, but you can work on putting anywhere. The important thing is to practice!

TENNIS BALL PUTTING

Try practice putting with a tennis ball from short distances. After doing so, the hole will look significantly larger to your eye when you go back to using a golf ball.

IN YOUR EYES

Lay a CD (don't use one from your favorite band, though!) upside-down on the ground and place a golf ball directly in the middle of it. When you take your stance over the ball, you should be able to see your eyes reflected in the CD. If you can't, then your head is not in the correct position. Turn back to page 121 and review the information on the putting stance.

THROUGH THE GATE

To help ensure that the center of your putter hits the ball, place the putter head on the ground and put a tee at each end of it. Remove the putter from between the tees and place a ball between them. Then practice hitting the ball with your putter without hitting the tees.

FIRM WRISTS

If you feel as if your wrists are breaking while you putt, try using the cross-handed grip (see page 120) during practice. Doing so helps you keep a firm left wrist and should prevent the putter head from getting ahead of your hands at impact.

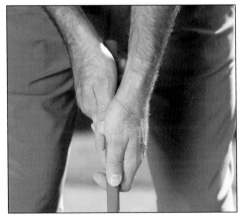

CONTINUED ON NEXT PAGE

DISTANCE CONTROL

To work on your distance control, place three tees in the ground—one 5 feet away, the next 2 feet to the right and 15 feet away, and the third another 2 feet to the right and 30 feet away from you. Alternate hitting putts to each tee to help develop your feel for distance.

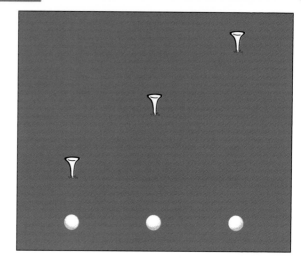

AROUND THE WORLD

Encircle a hole with balls at a short distance (say 3 feet) and move around the circle putting the balls into the hole. This repetitive drill will help you develop both feel and confidence on short putts. If you set up this drill on a hole that has a lot of slope, you will get a crash course in reading greens.

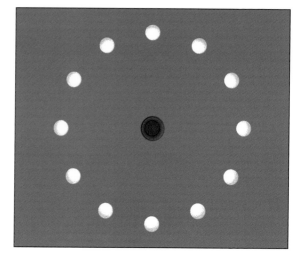

THE SWEET SPOT

Take two rubber bands and wrap them tightly around the center of the putter head about an inch apart. Then hit practice putts, making sure to strike the ball within the space between the two rubber bands. Doing so will help you target the sweet spot of the putter, which will likely create the best possible roll of the ball.

BACK AGAINST A CHAIR

Although you should keep your head steady while putting, you also need to keep your hips "quiet." Take your normal putting stance, but with your back pockets touching a chair, and then practice your putting stroke while maintaining contact with the chair. Doing so will help eliminate any lateral movement your hips might make and provide the feel of a very still and repeatable stroke.

TIP

Tempo is as important when putting as it is when making a full swing. Find a setting that clicks at the end of your backswing and then clicks again at the completion of your follow-through. Begin your backswing on one click, start your downswing on the next click, and finish your follow-through on the third click.

12

Review the Rules

Golf is defined by its rules. Short of memorizing the entire rule book, the United States Golf Association's *The Rules of Golf,* all golfers should understand some common situations. This chapter reviews these situations and discusses what you can and can't do in each one.

Yellow Stakes 172

Red Stakes 173

White Stakes 174

Lost and Found 175

On the Green 176

In a Bunker 177

Obstructions 178

Essential Golf Etiquette 180

Keep Score 184

A yellow stake indicates a water hazard on a fairway or in front of or behind a green. You have the following options if you hit a ball into an area marked with a yellow stake:

- Play the ball as it lies in the hazard, without penalty. Do this only if you can take your stance, make contact with the ball, and swing without endangering yourself.
- Play a new ball from behind the hazard, on a line between the hole and the point where the ball entered the hazard (a one-stroke penalty).
- Play a new ball from the spot from which you hit the original ball that entered the hazard (a one-stroke penalty).

A red stake indicates a lateral water hazard (a pond, lake, or stream located alongside a fairway or green). In a hazard defined by red stakes, you have two additional options, both of which carry a one-stroke penalty:

- Play a new ball up to two club lengths away—but no closer to the hole—from the point where the ball entered the hazard.
- Drop a ball no more than two club lengths away from the hazard in a spot equidistant from the flagstick on the other side of the hazard.

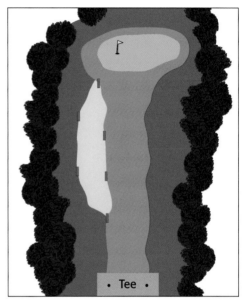

To make a proper drop, hold the ball at arm's length away from your body and level with your shoulder, and then release it to the ground.

A white stake indicates out of bounds, or an area from which you are not allowed to hit a ball. Courses also use property lines, such as a fence, to indicate out of bounds.

If your ball crosses into an area marked by white stakes, you must go back to the spot from which you originally hit and play another ball, taking a one-stroke penalty.

If you fear that you might not be able to find your ball after hitting it—for example, if you hit a slice into a wooded area—hit another ball (called a *provisional ball*) so that you don't have to walk all the way back to the original spot if your first ball doesn't turn up. Let your playing partners know that you are hitting a provisional ball.

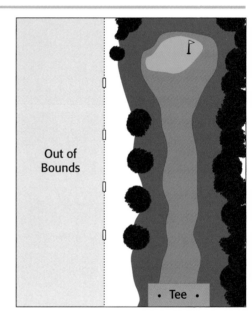

Out of Bounds

• Tee •

TIP

If you can't find your original ball and end up hitting a provisional ball, you incur a one-stroke penalty. Count one stroke for your original tee shot, one stroke for the lost ball penalty, and a third stroke for hitting a provisional ball.

Lost and Found

SEARCHING FOR A LOST BALL

According to the official rules, you are entitled to search for a lost ball for five minutes. If you don't find it within that time frame, you must return to the spot from which you originally hit it, play another ball, and record a penalty stroke. If you are playing a casual round and want to maintain a speedy pace of play, take a penalty stroke, drop a new ball as close as possible to where you think the ball was lost, and play from there.

HITTING THE WRONG BALL

Hitting the wrong ball during competition incurs a two-stroke penalty. You must go back and play your original ball if you have not yet completed the hole. In casual play, consider simply taking the penalty and moving on.

Always check to make sure that you are hitting your own ball. Marking the ball with your initials, a pattern of dots, or a symbol like the one shown here will help. Marking all your balls with the same unique mark prior to your round is a good idea.

CLEANING THE LINE OF A PUTT

You may use your hand or a towel to wipe away items on the line of your putt, including leaves and pebbles. You may repair ball marks, but you cannot repair spike marks caused by golf shoes.

TENDING THE FLAG

When all players have made it onto the putting surface, one person removes the flagstick and places it off to the side where it won't be in the way. However, one player may *tend the flag,* or hold the flagstick, while another player putts. This is often done on a large green when the person putting has an especially long putt and/or can't see the hole clearly from where the ball lies, or when someone chooses to putt from off the green.

If you are tending the flag for another player, you must remove it if the ball is rolling directly toward the hole. The person putting will incur a two-stroke penalty if the ball hits the pin while the flag is being tended.

GROUNDING YOUR CLUB

You cannot *ground your club* (let it touch the sand prior to hitting the ball) when playing a bunker shot unless you are in a designated *waste area* (a large, sandy area that is not maintained). You can hover the club directly behind the ball before such a shot, but grounding the club will incur a two-stroke penalty.

BALL RESTING AGAINST A RAKE

If your ball lands against a rake inside a bunker, carefully remove the rake. If the ball moves when you move the rake, you must return it to its original spot.

OBJECTS AFFECTING YOUR BALL OR STANCE

You may remove any artificial objects (such as plastic cups) that you find in a bunker affecting your ball or stance. However, you cannot move natural objects (such as leaves) that are near or touching the ball.

OBJECTS AFFECTING YOUR STANCE

If an object such as a storm drain or paved cart path interferes with your stance or swing, you are allowed to seek relief. Find the nearest point away from the obstacle to drop the ball, but do not drop the ball any closer to the hole.

OBJECTS AFFECTING THE BALL

If your ball is in the fairway or rough, you may remove a leaf or twig that is *covering* the ball. If doing so moves the ball, however, you incur a one-stroke penalty—so move the object very carefully! Remember that if the ball does move, you must return it to its original position or you will incur another penalty stroke.

If there is a leaf or twig *underneath* the ball, you must play the ball as it lies.

UNPLAYABLE LIE

If you find yourself unable to make any type of shot because of an obstruction—for example, if your ball has landed against the trunk of a tree—you have three options, each of which requires one penalty stroke:

1 Drop a ball within two club lengths of where your ball lies, but no closer to the hole.

2 Drop a ball behind the spot where your ball lies, going as far backward as you want but staying on a line directly between the hole and that spot.

3 Play the ball from as near as possible to where you last hit it.

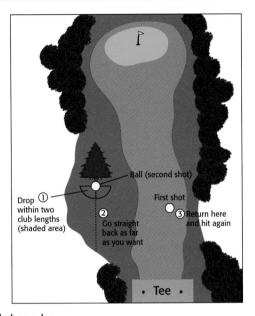

Ball (second shot)

First shot

Drop ① within two club lengths (shaded area)

② Go straight back as far as you want

③ Return here and hit again

· Tee ·

LIES DURING UNUSUAL CONDITIONS

If you're playing in poor conditions, you can use the lift, clean, and place rule:

- **Lift**: Pick up the ball after marking its location
- **Clean**: Wipe off dirt, grass, or moisture
- **Place**: Return the ball as close as possible (usually within 1 foot) to its original lie but no closer to the hole

Representatives of the course will determine whether this rule should be used. If you intend to post your score for handicap purposes, you must play by the rules declared by the course superintendent or head golf professional.

In addition to the official rules, keep in mind proper golf etiquette while you play. This section describes numerous situations you should know about.

ORDER OF PLAY

On the first tee, you need to choose who in your group will play first. That can be decided randomly; it is often done by throwing a tee into the air—whomever it points to goes first and so on until each person in the group has been assigned a spot.

The person who finishes with the lowest score on the first hole tees off first on the second hole. That person maintains "honors" until someone else shoots a lower score on a hole.

As you play, the person farthest from the hole always hits first. On the green, you can *putt out* (or continue to putt until the ball makes it into the hole) if you are not in someone else's putting line and the other players give you permission to do so. Otherwise, the person who is farthest from the hole putts next.

Always be ready to hit your shot as soon as the other players are done hitting. Do not wait until another player hits to plan your shot and choose a club. And don't make noise while other players hit!

PACE OF PLAY

The average time to play 18 holes is 4 hours and 15 minutes. Maintaining an efficient pace of play is important on every course. To avoid slow play:

- Always bring an extra club for the situation when walking to your ball.
- Plan your shot while others are hitting and be ready to hit when it's your turn.
- Write down your score on the next tee instead of on the green you just finished playing.
- Walk briskly.
- If you bring a club other than your putter to the green (such as a wedge), place it on or near the flagstick after it's removed from the hole—never off in the rough where it could be forgotten.
- Keep an eye on your ball and that of your playing partner; pick a tree, a bush, or another point to help you locate the ball.
- Hit an extra ball, known as a provisional ball, if you think your first ball might be lost.
- If no one is playing on the hole in front of you and the group behind you is waiting, let them play through if their group is smaller or faster than yours.
- In casual play, if the number of strokes you have taken on a hole is double the par of that hole, pick up your ball and move on to the next hole.
- Putt out. Marking your ball on the green and then re-marking it when it's your turn to hit takes a lot of time. Go ahead and finish, as long as you don't stand in someone else's line.

CART PATHS

If you are using a cart, always follow the signs on the course indicating where you can and cannot go. If you see signs indicating "Cart Paths Only," you can't drive the cart anywhere other than on those paths. A sign stating "Cart 90 Degrees Only" means that while you can drive the cart on the fairway, it must be at a 90-degree angle to the direction of the fairway at any given point. Never drive a cart on a tee box or green.

CONTINUED ON NEXT PAGE

REPLACING DIVOTS

Always replace the divot you leave after hitting a tee shot or fairway shot. Find the piece of grass that's likely in front of where you hit from and place it back in the bare spot you created. Today, most carts come with a container full of a mixture of sand and grass seed; simply spread the mixture over the divot and smooth it out.

RAKING THE SAND AFTER A BUNKER SHOT

Always rake the sand in a bunker as neatly as possible after you have hit a shot. Rake both the spot from which you hit the ball and any footprints you have made. Take note of where the rakes are placed and then return the rake you used to the same spot after you have finished raking the sand. Some courses keep the rakes inside the bunkers, while others place them just outside the bunkers.

REPAIRING BALL MARKS ON THE GREEN

Always repair any mark your ball might have made when landing on the green. Insert the divot repair tool into the ground around the edge of the mark and gently push toward the center of the mark. While you're at it, be a good Samaritan and fix ball marks made by other players, too.

MARKING YOUR BALL ON THE GREEN

Always mark your ball on the green when playing with others so that your ball does not block another player's path to the hole. If your mark is in another person's path, you can move the mark one putter clubhead length to the left or right of the original spot. Before you putt, return the ball to its original spot.

> ### TIP
>
> Never step on the putting line of another player, and do not stand behind or in front of another player on that line. If the person putting can see your foot while he or she is in position to hit the ball, then you are too close. Remember to be still and quiet while others are putting.

Every course provides a free scorecard for golfers to keep track of the strokes they take on each hole. You count one stroke for each attempt to hit the ball—even if you miss. The following categories receive their own space on a scorecard.

- **Hole number:** Shows the order in which holes are played. Usually one half of the scorecard shows holes 1–9, while the other side shows holes 10–18. This split enables you to fold the scorecard in half and place it in your pocket.

- **Yardage:** Represents the length of each hole. Scorecards often include multiple yardages for each hole, from the longest (referred to as the "back tees" or "tips") to the shortest ("forward tees"). Tees are assigned colors—usually black for the longest tees and red for the shortest. In this example, the course has four sets of tees.

- **Par:** Represents the number of strokes you should need to finish each hole.

- **Handicap or Strokes:** Ranks the difficulty of each hole in relation to how a bogey golfer would play it compared to a scratch golfer. For example, the hole ranked number 1 in the Handicap or Strokes box would be the one that a bogey golfer would need the most help with when competing against a scratch golfer; the hole ranked 18th, the least.

  Handicap strokes are also applied using these rankings. If you are a 15 handicap, you receive one stroke each on the holes numbered 1–15 in this category. If your handicap is higher than 18, you apply one stroke to every hole and then add any remaining strokes to holes in order of handicap ranking. For example, if your handicap is 24, you would apply two strokes each to holes ranked 1 through 6 in the Handicap category; all others would receive one stroke. If you are playing against another player, you simply subtract the better player's handicap from the lesser player's handicap. For example, if you are a 24 handicap playing against a 10 handicap, you receive one stroke on the 14 holes ranked 1–14 in the Handicap or Strokes category.

- **Score box:** The area in which you record the number of strokes you took on each hole. There is usually enough room on a scorecard to track four players' scores.

HOLE	BLACK	BLUE	STROKES					PAR			STROKES	WHITE	RED
1	538	513	7					5			1	491	469
2	389	378	9					4			11	356	340
3	177	159	17					3			17	144	126
4	435	418	1					4			5	393	367
5	500	489	11					5			7	471	417
6	392	375	15					4			13	341	315
7	217	206	13					3			15	173	161
8	528	512	3					5			3	482	464
9	440	410	5					4			9	347	276
OUT	3616	3457						37				3198	2935
10	390	362	10					4			12	337	314
11	197	175	16					3			16	158	125
12	601	579	2					5			2	553	526
13	417	375	4					4			10	354	318
14	157	138	18					3			18	121	89
15	521	502	6					5			8	485	444
16	359	337	12					4			4	307	289
17	247	191	14					3			14	170	150
18	414	394	8					4			6	356	325
IN	3303	3053						35				2841	2580
TOT	6919	6510						72				6039	5515
HANDICAP													
NET SCORE													
DATE		SCORER				ATTEST							

Games You Can Play

In addition to *stroke play* (whoever finishes with the fewest strokes wins) or *match play* (where a hole is either won or tied, known as *halved*), you can play or use numerous other games and scoring formats on the course. Besides providing another competitive outlet, each game can help you stay involved in your round no matter how well or poorly you're playing. And they're fun!

Alternate Shot: In this format, two players form a team and hit alternate shots on each hole. If Player A hits the tee shot, Player B hits the next shot, and so on.

Best Ball: A popular outing format in which all players in a foursome play their own ball, with the lowest score (or "best ball") counting as the team's score for that hole.

Bingo Bango Bongo: A format that puts separate values on a player's long game, short game, and putting. On each hole, 3 points are available to win: The first point goes to the player who reaches the green in the fewest strokes; the second point goes to the player who is closest to the pin after everyone is on the green; and the final point is awarded to the player who gets the ball into the hole in the fewest strokes overall.

Four Ball: Used when playing in a foursome, this format pits the best ball (lowest score) of one twosome against the best ball of the other twosome.

Nassau: This form of match-play betting involves separate wagers on the front nine score, the back nine score, and the overall result of the match. For example, if Player A is two up through nine holes, he or she wins the front nine. If Player A then loses the back nine one down, he or she loses the wager for that nine. The overall score has Player A winning one up over 18 holes.

Points: This game involves the awarding of points to players on each hole, depending on their scores. For example, if you're playing in a threesome, 9 points could be available on every hole; the best score gets 5 points, the second best gets 3 points, and the third best gets 1 point. If all players get the same score for the hole, each one gets 3 points.

Sandies/Greenies: Also referred to as "garbage"; points are awarded for *sandies* (when a player takes one shot out of a bunker and then one putt on the green—in some versions, the putt has to be for par) and *greenies* (awarded to the closest player to the pin on a hole—usually only on par-threes). The player with the most points in each of those categories, or a combined total, wins.

Scramble: The most frequently used format for outings has all players in the group hit tee shots. The best drive of the group is then selected, and all players hit from that point; the best of those shots is selected, and all players hit from there. This process continues until the ball is in the hole. Usually a minimum of three drives from each player in the group must be used within 18 holes.

Shamble: In this fun outing format, all players hit tee shots and the best is picked; then all players play their own balls from that point into the hole.

Skins: This format puts a prize ("skin") on each hole, with the lowest score winning the skin. If there is no single lowest score, that skin carries over to the next hole, and so on. Whoever ends up with the most skins at the end of the round wins the predetermined reward. It's a great game for beginners because each hole is its own separate match.

Stableford: In this format, point values are assigned to each type of score per hole (eagle, birdie, par, bogey, and so on). Each player accumulates points based on how well he or she does relative to par. The player with the most points at the end of the round wins.

Wolf: Wolf is typically a three-player game in which players alternate who plays against the others on each hole. On each tee, a designated player chooses who his or her partner will be for the hole, with the better ball (or lowest score) of those two players matched up against the best ball of the remaining player in the group.

Glossary

ace   A hole-in-one.

address   The stance in which you are ready to strike the ball.

approach   A shot taken with the intention of reaching the green.

apron   The closely mown area located in front of the putting surface.

away   The player whose ball is farthest from the hole is considered "away" and should play his or her shot next, before all others who are closer to the hole.

back nine   Usually the holes numbered 10–18 on a course, or the last nine holes played in a competitive round. Some courses start players off on the tenth tee, making holes 10–18 the front nine and holes 1–9 the back nine.

backswing   The first portion of the swing, in which the club moves from address to the top.

bent grass   A type of grass used on putting greens.

Bermuda grass   A type of grass used on putting greens. It is more resistant to heat than bent grass and also reflects more grain, which affects the way you read a green: If you are putting against the grain, the grass will look darker; if you are putting with the grain, the grass will look shiny and the ball will roll more quickly.

birdie   A score of one stroke less than the assigned par for a hole.

bite   A term that describes the way a ball lands on the green and stops suddenly due to backspin.

blading   Hitting the ball with the bottom edge of a club.

blind shot   A shot in which you cannot see your intended landing area.

bogey   A score of one stroke more than the assigned par for a hole.

break   The amount of movement, or curvature, between your ball and the hole. The topography of a putting surface can force the ball to move in different directions.

bump and run   A shot in which the ball lands on the ground soon after leaving the clubface and rolls toward the target.

bunker   A depression in the ground usually filled with sand (though sometimes with grass), found mostly around greens but also in and along fairways. Bunkers are intended to trap errant shots.

caddy   The person who carries your golf clubs during a round (and is usually paid for the effort). A caddy can also keep your clubs clean, provide yardages for shots, rake bunkers, and help you read greens.

carry   The distance a ball travels in the air.

cast   A type of clubhead made by pouring metal into a mold.

casual water   Standing water on the course that is outside a normal water hazard; typically a temporary situation, normally the result of rain or a sprinkler system.

check   To quickly stop rolling on the green due to backspin.

chip   A low, rolling shot that travels farther on the ground than it does in the air. This shot is used to advance the ball a short distance (35 yards or less) onto the green from the fairway or the fringe around the green. You can also chip from the rough if you have a good lie.

choke down   To move your hands from the end of the grip downward toward the lower portion of the grip.

closed   A position in which the clubface can end up when it impacts the ball. A closed clubface usually causes the ball to move left. The term *closed* also refers to a type of stance.

clubface The portion of the clubhead that is designed to make contact with the ball.

clubhead The part of the club that hits the ball; it is connected to the shaft by the hosel.

clubhouse The central building at a golf facility where you pay green fees; the club-house usually includes the pro shop, locker rooms, and restaurant.

collar Where the fringe of the putting surface meets the rough.

concede To allow your opponent to pick up the ball during match play when he or she has a short putt that you do not believe will be missed. By conceding the putt (or the hole itself at any time), you do not require your opponent to actually make the putt or finish playing the hole.

cup The cylindrical hole in the green that supports the flagstick.

divot A portion of turf torn from the ground by a golf swing; also refers to the mark left in the ground as a result.

dogleg A par-four or par-five hole that bends dramatically to the right or left.

downswing The portion of the swing where the club moves from its highest point to impact with the ball.

draw A shot that curves from right to left in a controlled manner.

drive The first shot on a par-four or par-five hole for which a driver is used.

drive the green A rare situation in which a tee shot reaches the green on a par-four or par-five.

driving range A stand-alone facility or an area of a golf course where you can hit prac-tice shots.

drop area A designated area on a golf course where you can drop a ball after hitting it into a water hazard or an environmentally sensitive area; usually identified by a sign.

eagle   A score of two strokes less than the assigned par for a hole.

fade   A shot that curves from left to right in a controlled manner.

fairway   The closely mown turf that stretches between the tee and the green.

false front   A deceptive design feature used by course architects to make a green appear closer than it really is. The false front extends into the fairway, usually in a downward fashion, often causing golfers to misjudge the distance and hit balls short of the proper landing area.

fat   A term used to describe hitting the ground first and then the ball, causing the ball to travel a shorter distance than planned.

first cut   The portion of rough immediately adjacent to the fairway.

flagstick   The stick placed in the hole on each green. A flag is attached to the top of the stick to help players see the position of the hole from far away. Also known as the *pin*.

flop shot   A high, arcing shot that lands softly with little roll. It is used mainly around greens to fly over bunkers or to reach a pin that is close to the near edge of the green.

follow-through   The portion of the swing that occurs after the clubhead makes impact with the ball.

fore   The term shouted by golfers after they hit an off-target shot to warn other players of the approaching ball.

forged   The clubhead-making process in which a block of solid metal is shaved down to a certain shape; forged clubs are usually the most expensive type.

foursome   A group comprised of four golfers. Golf facilities typically prefer that people play in groups of four, especially when the course is busy.

free drop   A situation in which you can move the ball and drop it without penalty—for example, if your ball ends up in an area marked as "ground under repair."

fringe   A portion of closely mown turf that encircles the putting surface; fringe grass is slightly higher than the green.

front nine   Usually the holes numbered 1–9 on a golf course, or the first nine holes played in a competitive round. Some courses start players off on the tenth tee, making holes 1–9 the back nine.

gallery   The people watching a golf tournament in person.

gap wedge   A highly lofted club (50 to 54 degrees) that fills the gap between the pitching wedge and sand wedge.

gimme   A short putt that is expected to be made.

green   The designated putting surface of each hole, where the pin and cup are located.

green fee   The amount a facility charges for playing a round of golf.

grip   The material, usually rubber or leather, wrapped around the top of a club. This term is also used to describe your hold on the club.

ground the club   To rest your club on the ground prior to making a swing. Grounding your club in a bunker is not permitted.

ground under repair   An area on a golf course usually marked by a sign or by lines painted on the ground. If your ball ends up inside such an area, you are allowed to pick it up and drop it outside of the area, but no closer to the hole, without incurring a penalty stroke.

halve   To record the same score as another player on a hole in match play; that hole is said to be halved. This term also refers to a match that ends in a draw.

handicap   A number created by converting your established Handicap Index into an appropriate *Course Handicap* (a number that indicates a golfer's ability level—the better you are, the lower this number will be) for each course you play.

Handicap Index   According to the USGA, "The number issued by your golf club, which represents your potential scoring ability; it is expressed as a number taken to one decimal place (i.e., 10.4)." This index enables golfers with different scoring abilities and skill levels to play one another and have a competitive match. Use the chart available at the course you are playing to convert your Handicap Index into a Course Handicap.

hazard   An obstacle on the course, such as water (pond, lake, stream) or sand (bunker), that can add extra strokes to your score, either via a penalty stroke or because additional shots are needed to exit the hazard.

head cover   An item typically found on drivers and woods that protects the clubhead and the shaft of the club while the club is not in use.

heel   The end of the clubface that is closer to the shaft.

hole   See *cup*.

hole-in-one   The rare situation in which you take a total of one stroke to get the ball from the tee into the hole. Also known as an *ace*.

hole out   To finish a hole by knocking the ball into the cup.

honors   The right to tee off first. Whoever has the lowest score on a hole is assigned the "honors" of teeing off first on the next hole.

hook   An errant shot that curves sharply from right to left in an uncontrolled manner.

hosel   The part of a golf club that connects the shaft with the clubhead; sometimes referred to as the *neck*.

hybrid   A golf club that blends elements of an iron and a fairway wood.

impact   The moment the clubhead makes contact with the ball.

iron   The name for a club other than a driver, wood, or putter, numbered 1–9, plus the pitching wedge, sand wedge, and lob wedge.

lag   A long putt not expected to be made, but that finishes close enough to the hole that the following putt is very makeable.

lateral water hazard   Defined by red stakes, a hazard found to the side of a fairway or green.

lay up   To hit the ball short of the target rather than try to cover the entire distance. A golfer typically makes this shot selection when facing a long distance to cover in order to decrease the margin of error.

leader board   A chart posted during a golf tournament to show which players are leading the event.

lie   The position of your ball on the ground.

lift, clean, and place   A rule applied during a round in which bad weather conditions are in effect; it allows players to pick up the ball, clean it, and place it on a better lie without penalty.

links course   A wide-open, usually treeless style of golf course; an authentic links course is built on sandy soil very close to the sea.

lip   The edge of a hole.

lob wedge   A highly lofted club (at least 58 degrees or more) used to hit the ball a short distance with great height.

loft   The angle of the clubface relative to the ground, measured in degrees. The greater the degree of loft, the higher the trajectory and the shorter the distance of the club.

loose impediment   A natural object not deemed to be an integral part of the course, such as a pinecone, twig, or leaf. You may remove loose impediments that affect your shot or stance without penalty unless in a bunker or hazard.

marker   An object used to mark the position of the ball on the green. You use a marker when your ball is in the way of another player's putt or when you want to pick up the ball to clean it.

marshal   The person whose job is to monitor the play of a particular hole, usually during a tournament.

match play   A competitive format in which one player (or team) competes against another, with individual scores determining who wins each hole. When one player (or team) has won more holes than there are holes left to play (e.g., the player is up five holes with four left to play), that player (or team) wins the match.

misread   To fail to understand the topography of the green, resulting in a missed putt.

movable obstruction   According to the USGA's *The Rules of Golf*, "Something (except for objects defining out of bounds or objects out of bounds) that may be moved without unreasonable effort, without unduly delaying play, and without causing damage to the course." Such objects include rakes, coffee cups, trash cans, and benches.

mulligan   An unofficial tradition of taking another shot if the first one is not to your liking. Mulligans are not accepted under the official rules of golf.

offset   A clubhead whose leading edge is positioned behind the hosel.

open   A position in which the clubface can end up when it impacts the ball. An open clubface usually results in the ball moving to the right.

pairing   The person or people with whom you are assigned to play.

par   The number of strokes a scratch golfer (one with a Course Handicap of zero) should take to complete a hole.

penalty stroke   An additional shot added to the score on a hole due to various rule situations, such as hitting a ball out of bounds or in a hazard, losing a ball, or grounding a club in a bunker.

pin   Also known as the *flagstick,* the target placed in each hole on the course. A flag is attached to the top of the pin to help players see its location from a distance.

pin-high   An approach shot that comes to rest perpendicular to the pin. A pin-high shot can be on or off the green.

pitch   A shot hit from around or close to the green that travels more through the air than it does on the ground. This shot helps your ball fly over bunkers, water, or rough to get close to the hole. Because you use a high-lofted club to play this shot, the ball retains extra spin, giving it both height and the ability to stop quickly once it lands instead of rolling along the green as a chip shot would.

pitching wedge   A club with a loft of 48 degrees, used for pitch shots.

play through   To move ahead of players on a hole to improve the pace of play. Proper etiquette calls for faster players to play through slower players after asking permission to do so.

practice green   A putting surface (not part of the course itself) where you can practice putts prior to or after your round.

private course   A golf course that requires membership to play.

pro-am   An event, usually held the day before a tournament begins, in which professionals play with amateurs who have paid to participate.

pro shop   A golf course facility, often located within the clubhouse, where you pay green fees, reserve tee times, pay for practice balls, and buy food and merchandise.

provisional ball   A second ball hit when you think your original ball might be lost or out-of-bounds.

public course   A golf course that is open to the public and does not require membership to play.

pull   A shot that travels directly left of your target after impact.

punch out   To use an abbreviated backswing to move the ball into a better position and out of trouble. Punching out is often required when the ball is in heavy rough, underneath a tree, or in tall grass.

push   A shot that travels directly right of your target after impact.

putt   A stroke you take when the ball is on the green.

putt out   To finish putting, even if your ball is not the one farthest from the hole.

range finder   A device used to calculate the yardage of a shot (not always allowed in tournaments).

ranger   The person whose primary job is to ensure the proper pace of play on a golf course and oversee the needs of the players. Also called a *marshal.*

read the green   To analyze the shape and topography of the putting surface in order to control the speed and accuracy of a putt.

red stake   Indicates a lateral water hazard located to the side of a fairway or green.

regulation   The number of strokes required to land the ball on the putting surface within par minus two strokes (in one shot on a par-three, in two shots on a par-four, or in three shots on a par-five).

release   When the ball hits the ground and moves forward; or to rotate the right hand over the left hand during the swing, which helps square the clubface.

relief   Depending on the situation, a player can move his or her ball to a more favorable position, known as obtaining relief, with or without a penalty (for example, when a ball stops on a cart path or lands behind a tree).

rough   High and often thick grass that borders the fairway and surrounds the green.

round   Eighteen holes of golf (or nine holes on a nine-hole course).

sand wedge   A highly lofted club (54 to 57 degrees) used to hit shots out of bunkers, short-distance shots from the fairway to the green, or shots from heavy rough.

scratch golfer   A player with a zero handicap—that is, a really good player.

second cut   A type of rough that is adjacent to the first cut but is higher and often thicker.

semiprivate course   A course that is open to the public but also offers memberships.

shaft   The part of the club that connects the grip with the clubhead. It can be made of graphite or steel.

shank   An errant shot hit off the hosel of the club; it usually travels almost 90 degrees to the right.

short game   Collectively, the shots made on, close to, or around the green.

short-sided   A term used to describe a player who has missed the green to the side that gives him or her the least amount of putting surface on which to land a pitch shot.

shotgun start   A format used during a golf outing in which foursomes are assigned to various holes and start play at the same time.

skulled shot   A shot that stays low to the ground and does not go in the direction you're aiming.

slice   An errant shot that curves sharply from left to right in an uncontrolled manner.

sole   The underside of a club.

spin   An important factor affecting the trajectory, distance, and accuracy of a golf shot. The angle of the club's impact imparts spin on the ball.

starter   The person positioned near the first tee at a golf course who assists players in beginning their rounds in a timely manner; also acts as the caddy master.

stroke   A swing taken with the intention of advancing the ball.

stroke play   A widely used competitive format in which your score equals the total number of strokes you have taken; the player with the fewest strokes wins. Also known as *medal play.*

superintendent   The person responsible for the maintenance of the course and grounds at a golf facility.

sweet spot   The center of the clubface.

swing plane   The path along which your club travels during the swing.

tap-in   A short putt that requires a simple tap to knock the ball into the hole.

tee   The closely mown, often raised section of a hole from which you hit your first shot on the hole. Also, a small object with a point at the bottom that is used to raise the ball up off the surface of the tee box.

tee markers   A pair of items that define the proper teeing area on each hole. You must tee up your ball between the markers or no more than two club lengths behind them.

tee shot   The first shot on a par-four or par-five hole for which a club other than a driver is used. If you use a driver, this shot is called a *drive*.

tend the flag   To hold the flagstick, or pin, while another player putts, often done on a large green or when someone putts from off the green.

thin   A term used to describe striking the middle or equator of the ball with the leading edge of the club, causing it to stay low to the ground with very little spin.

tight   Close to the hole.

toe   The end of the clubface that is farthest from the shaft.

top   To strike the top half of the ball with the leading edge of the club, causing topspin and forcing the ball to fall to the ground immediately rather than travel up into the air.

turn   The point at which you have completed the first nine holes of a course (the *front nine*) and are ready to begin the second nine holes (the *back nine*).

unplayable lie   A lie in which the ball has come to rest in a position (such as behind a large rock) from which it cannot be hit.

up and down   A two-shot sequence that typically occurs around the green after the approach shot has missed the green or landed in a bunker. The first shot is hit "up" onto the green, and the first putt then goes "down" into the hole. Also referred to as a *save*.

waggle   The process of moving the club back and forth just prior to hitting the ball, which helps loosen up your arms and shoulders.

waste area   A large, sandy area on a golf course that is not maintained by the groundskeeping staff.

water hazard   A pond, stream, or other body of water on a golf course defined by yellow or red stakes.

wedge   A lofted club used for short-distance shots approaching the green.

whiff   To swing a club with the intention of hitting the ball but to miss it completely. A whiff counts as a stroke.

white stake   Indicates an area that is out-of-bounds.

winter rules   A local rule put into effect in poor conditions, usually implemented during the winter months, allowing golfers to improve the position of the ball between the tee and the green without penalty. Also known as *preferred lies.*

wood   A club with a large head made of wood or metal that is used for tee shots and long fairway shots. Woods are numbered 1, 3, and 5; 7 and 9 woods with greater loft are also available.

yardage marker   Indicates the distance, in yards, from a certain point to the green. A yardage marker might reflect the distance to the front, center, or back of the green; if only one number appears, it refers to the center of the green. Yardage markers are placed on the fairway or on the cart path; yardages can also be marked on sprinkler heads.

yellow stake   Indicates a water hazard on the course.

yips   A condition that afflicts players who can't keep their hands and arms steady while putting (and sometimes chipping), resulting in consistently poor shots.

Index

A

ace, 188
address, 188
aligning your shot, 40, 41, 42
Alternate Shot game, 186
approach, 188
apron, 188
Around the World drill, 168
away, defined, 188

B

Back Against a Chair drill, 169
back nine, 188
backswing
 of chip shots, 92
 defined, 188
 of drives, 51–52
 of greenside bunker shots, 106
 for hitting against the collar, 79
 for hitting off downhill lie, 85
 for hitting off uphill lie, 86
 for hitting under tree, 82
 of iron shots, 63–67
 of pitch shots, 100
 of putts, 125, 126
balls
 lost, 175
 marker on green for, 116, 183, 195
 marking before round, 175
 objects affecting, 177–178
 overview, 12
 positioning, 39, 60
baseball grip, 33
bent grass, 188
Bermuda grass, 188
Best Ball game, 186
Bingo Bango Bongo game, 186
birdie, 188
bite, 188
blade putter, 10
blading, 189
blind shot, 189
bogey, 189
break, 189
bump and run, 189

bunker
 defined, 189
 entering properly, 105
 raking after shot, 182
 removing objects in, 177
 sand quality in, 107
Bunker Balance drill, 165
bunker shots
 ball resting against rake, 177
 drills, 163–165
 fairway, 110, 111–113, 164
 greenside, 104–109, 111–113, 163–164
 grounding your club, 108, 177, 192
 for various lies, 111–112
buried lie, 111

C

caddy, 189
carry, 189
cart paths, 181
cast irons, 7, 189
casual water, 189
cavity-back irons, 7
check, 189
chipping
 clubs for, 90
 defined, 90, 189
 drills, 159–162
 from fairway, 93
 follow-through, 91
 from rough, 94
 stance, 91
 swing, 92
choke down, 189. See also gripping
classic putter, 10
claw putter grip, 120
cleaning line of putt, 176
closed clubface
 defined, 189
 problems, 43, 66, 74, 75, 139
clubface. See also closed clubface; open clubface
 defined, 190
 maintenance, 11
 squaring, 43
clubhead, 4, 190

clubs. *See also specific kinds*
    for chipping, 90
    distance charts for, 14–15
    fitting for, 11
    for greenside bunker shots, 110
    maintenance, 11
    parts of, 4
    for pitching, 95
collar, 79, 190
concede, 190
Correct Your Weight Shift drill, 142–143
cross-handed putter grip, 120
cup
    defined, 190
    studying angle of, 128

D

distance charts for clubs, 14–15
Distance Control drill, 168
Divot Directions drill, 155
divots
    defined, 190
    direction of, 155
    in fairway bunker shots, 110
    hitting out of, 78
    learning from, 154
    replacing, 182
dogleg, 190
Dollar's Worth drill, 165
downhill lie, 85, 113
downhill putts, 130
downswing
    defined, 68, 190
    of drives, 52
    of iron shots, 68
draws
    aligning, 41
    closed clubface for, 43
    defined, 41, 190
    hooks versus, 139
    purpose of, 42
    strong grip for, 34
drills. *See also* practice
    bunker shots, 163–165
    chipping and pitching, 159–162
    driving, 150–153
    fat shot correction, 142–143
    hitting thin, fixing, 144–145
    hook correction, 140–141, 152
    iron shots, 154–158
    line drive correction, 147
    pop-up correction, 146, 152
    putting, 166–169
    slice correction, 135–138, 152
    topping correction, 144–145
drive, 190
drivers
    deciding to use, or not, 55
    head covers for, 6
    overview, 5
drive the green, 190
driving
    drills, 150–153
    keys to good swing, 49
    making the swing, 50–54
    positioning the ball for, 39
    targets for practicing, 24
    teeing the ball, 46
    tee shot routine, 56–57
    using the tee box, 47–48
    warming up, 23
driving range, 23, 24, 190
drop area, 190

E

eagle, 191
etiquette, 180–183

F

fades
    aligning, 42
    defined, 42, 191
    open clubface for, 43
    purpose of, 42
    slices versus, 134
    weak grip for, 34
fairway
    bunker shots, 110, 111–113, 164
    chipping from, 93
    defined, 191
    putting from, 131
    reading the green from, 128
fairway woods
    deciding to use, or not, 55
    head covers for, 6
    overview, 6
    positioning the ball for, 39
false front, 191
fat shots, 83, 142–143, 191
Feet Together drill, 144–145

finish. *See also* follow-through
of drives, 54
of greenside bunker shots, 109
of iron shots, 72
of pitch shots, 101
Firm Wrists drill, 167
First Base drill, 153
first cut, 191
fitting
clubs, 11
grips, 33
putter, 123
flagstick, 176, 191
flop shot, 191
follow-through. *See also* finish
of chip shots, 91
defined, 191
of drives, 53–54
of greenside bunker shots, 109
for hitting under tree, 82
of iron shots, 71
of putts, 126
fore, 191
forged irons, 7, 191
Four Ball game, 186
foursome, 191
free drop, 191
fringe, 131, 191
front nine, 192
Full Extension drill, 156
Futura putter, 10

G

gallery, 192
games and scoring formats, 186–187
gap wedge, 9, 192
gimme, 192
green
defined, 192
repairing ball marks on, 183
green fee, 192
greenside bunker shots
backswing, 106
clubs for, 110
drills, 163–164
follow-through, 109
grounding your club, 108
handling various lies, 111–113
impact, 107–108
stance, 105

grip
to avoid hitting to the right, 35
baseball type, 33
consistent pressure for, 31
defined, 4, 192
fitting to hand size, 33
hand placements, 34–35
for hitting off downhill, 85
for hitting off sidehill, 83, 84
for hitting off uphill, 86
for hitting under tree, 82
interlocking type, 32
left hand, 28–29
maintenance, 11, 29
matching to your shot, 31
options available, 28
overlapping type, 32
for putting, 119–120
right hand, 30
testing the pressure, 31
grounding your club, 108, 177, 192
ground under repair, 192–193

H

halved hole, 186, 192
handicap, 192
Handicap Index, 192
handicap strokes, 184
Hands Ahead drill, 162
Hands drill, 136–137
hazard, 193
head cover, 5, 6, 193
Hear the Swoosh drill, 150
heel, 4, 193
High Tee drill, 146, 152
Hit the Line drill, 163
hole. *See* cup
hole-in-one, 193
hole out, 193
honors, 193
hooks
causes, 34, 43, 66, 74, 75, 139
defined, 139, 193
draws versus, 139
drills, 140–141, 152
fixing, 139–141
pulls versus, 139
hosel, 4, 193

hybrid clubs
    deciding to use, or not, 55
    defined, 8, 193
    positioning the ball for, 39

I

impact
    of bunker shots, 107–108
    of chip shots, 92
    defined, 193
    of drives, 53
    flight path due to, 73
    when hitting under tree, 82
    of iron shots, 69–70
    of pitch shots, 101
    of putts, 125–126
    tape showing, 70
Impact drill, 141
In-n-Out drill, 152
inside-outside swing path, 75, 139
interlocking grip type, 32
In Your Eyes drill, 166
irons. *See also* wedges
    deciding to use, or not, 55
    defined, 193
    overview, 7
iron shots
    backswing, 63–67
    downswing, 68
    drills, 154–158
    finish, 72
    follow-through, 71
    impact, 69–70
    positioning the ball for, 39, 60
    practice swing for, 62
    re-establishing comfort level for, 67
    stance for, 61
    swing path, 73–75
    three-quarter swing for practicing, 70

K

keeping score, 184–185

L

lag, 193
lateral water hazard, 193
lay up, 194
leader board, 194
Learn from Your Divots drill, 154
lie, 194. *See also* tricky lies

lift, clean, and place rule, 179, 194
line drives, correcting, 147
links course, 194
lip, 194
lob wedge
    defined, 9, 194
    for greenside bunker shots, 104
    for pitching, 95
loft
    defined, 5, 194
    of drivers, 5, 55
    for greenside bunker shots, 104
    for hitting off downhill lie, 85
    for hitting off sidehill lie, 83, 84
    for hitting off uphill lie, 86
    of irons, 7, 62, 69
    of wedges, 9
    of woods, 6
loose impediment, 177–178, 194
lost ball, 175
Low Ceiling drill, 153

M

maintenance, 11, 29
marker for ball, 116, 183, 194
marshal, 194
match play, 186, 194
misread, 195
Miss the Back Ball drill, 162
Miss the Bucket drill, 138, 140
Miss the Tees drill, 160
movable obstruction, 177–178, 195
mulligan, 195

N

Nassau game, 186
neutral grip, 34, 35

O

obstructions, rules for, 177–178
Odyssey Two Ball putter, 10
offset irons, 7, 195
One-Arm Swings drill, 161
open clubface
    defined, 195
    for hitting off sidehill lie, 84
    for hitting out of rough, 80
    problems, 43, 50, 66, 74, 75, 134
order of play, 180

outside-inside swing path
  drill, 152
  for hitting out of divot, 78
  for hitting out of rough, 81
  problems, 74
overlapping grip, 32

P

pace of play, 181
pairing, 195
par, 184, 195
penalty strokes
  defined, 195
  for grounding your club, 108, 177
  for hitting wrong ball, 175
  for lost ball, 175
  for hitting provisional ball, 174
  for putting into pin, 176
  in red stake areas, 173
  for unplayable lie, 179
  in white stake areas, 174
  in yellow stake areas, 172
pin
  defined, 195
  hitting on putt, 176
pin-high, 195
pitching
  clubs for, 95
  defined, 95, 195
  drills, 159–162
  high-trajectory, 99
  low-trajectory, 97
  medium-trajectory, 98
  putting versus, 95
  stance, 96–99
  swing, 100–101
pitching wedge, 9, 95, 195
play through, 196
Points game, 186
pop-ups, 146, 152
positioning the ball, 39, 60
posture. See stance
Posture drill, 157
practice. See also drills
  hitting odd or even clubs, 24
  iron shots, 70
  playing holes, 25
  with purpose, 24–25
  short game, 25
  using targets for driving, 24

practice green, 22, 196
practice swing, 62, 121
private course, 196
pro-am, 196
pro shop, 196
provisional ball, 174, 196
public course, 196
pulls
  defined, 196
  drill, 152
  hooks versus, 139
  from open clubface, 66
  from strong grip, 35
punch out, 196
pushes
  from closed clubface, 66
  defined, 196
  grip for avoiding, 35
  slices versus, 134
putter, 10
putting
  cleaning line of putt, 176
  controlling the distance, 129–131
  defined, 196
  downhill, 130
  drills, 166–169
  etiquette, 183
  exhaling before stroke, 118
  from fairway, 131
  from fringe, 131
  gripping the putter, 119–120
  long, 129
  making the swing, 125–126
  out, 180
  pitching versus, 95
  practice swing for, 121
  reading the green, 117, 127–128, 197
  routine for, 116–118
  stance, 121–124
  uphill, 130
  warming up, 22
putt out, 196

R

raking after bunker shot, 182
range finder, 196
ranger, 197
reading the green, 117, 127–128, 197
red stakes, 173, 197
regulation, 197

release, 197
relief, 197
repairing ball marks on green, 183
replacing divots, 182
rough, 80–81, 94, 197
round, 197
routine
    for putting, 116–118
    for tee shot, 56–57
rules
    in bunkers, 177
    cleaning line of putt, 176
    etiquette, 180–183
    grounding your club, 177
    hitting wrong ball, 175
    lift, clean, and place, 179
    obstructions, 177–178
    red stakes, 173, 197
    score keeping, 184–185
    searching for lost ball, 175
    tending the flag, 176
    unplayable lie, 179
    white stakes, 174, 201
    yellow stakes, 172, 201

S

Sandies/Greenies game, 187
sand wedge, 9, 95, 104, 197
score keeping, 184–185
Scotty Cameron Detour putter, 10
scramble, 187
scratch golfer, 197
second cut, 197
semiprivate course, 197
Shadow Knows drill, 151
shaft, 4, 197
Shamble game, 187
shank, 198
short game, 25, 198
short-sided, 198
shotgun start, 198
Shoulders drill, 135
sidehill lie, hitting off of, 83–84
Skins game, 187
skulled shots, 147, 198
slices
    advantages limited for, 134
    causes, 34, 43, 50, 66, 74, 75, 134
    defined, 134, 198
    drills, 135–138, 152

    fades versus, 134
    fixing, 134–138
    pushes versus, 134
    tee box position for tendency, 48
sole, 198
spin, 198
Splash Around drill, 163
squaring the clubface, 43
Stableford game, 187
stance
    aligning your shot, 40–42
    bunker shots, 105, 110, 112–113
    chipping, 91
    driving, 50
    hitting off downhill lie, 85, 113
    hitting off sidehill lie, 83, 84
    hitting off uphill lie, 86, 112
    improper, 38
    iron shots, 61
    objects affecting, 177–178
    pitching, 96–99
    positioning the ball within, 39
    practicing before mirror, 38
    proper, 36–37
    putting, 121–124
    squaring the clubface, 43
Stand on Glass drill, 164
starter of golf course, 198
starter set of clubs, 7, 9, 11, 104
stretching, 18–21
stroke, 198
stroke play, 186, 198
strong grip, 34, 35, 139
superintendent, 198
sweet spot, 4, 198
Sweet Spot drill, 169
swing path or swing plane
    defined, 198
    drills, 152–153
    inside-outside, 75, 139
    of iron shots, 73–75
    outside-inside, 74, 78, 81, 152

T

tap-in, 198
tee box, 47–48, 184
teeing the ball, 46, 55
Tee It Up drill, 164
tee markers, 199
tees, 13, 199

tee shot. *See also* driving
    defined, 199
    routine for, 56–57
    teeing the ball, 46
    using the tee box, 47–48
tending the flag, 176, 199
Tennis Ball Putting drill, 166
thin shots, 144–145, 199
Through the Gate drill, 167
tight, 199
toe, 4, 199
topping, 144–145, 199
tree, hitting out from under, 82
tricky lies
    against the collar, 79
    deep rough, 80–81
    in divot, 78
    downhill, 85, 113
    sidehill, 83–84
    under tree, 82
    uphill, 86–87, 112
troubleshooting
    fat shots, 142–143
    hitting thin or topping, 144–145
    hooks, 139–141
    line drives, 147
    pop-ups, 146
    slices, 134–138
turn, 199

U

Unbreakable drill, 159
unplayable lie, 179, 199

up and down, 199
uphill lie, 86–87, 112
uphill putts, 130

W

waggle, 199
warming up
    stretching, 18–21
    using practice areas, 22–23
waste area, 199
water hazard, 200
weak grip, 34
wedges. *See also* specific kinds
    defined, 200
    overview, 9
    for pitching, 95
    positioning the ball for, 39, 60
Weight Transfer drill, 158
Where's Your Left Elbow? drill, 158
whiff, 200
white stakes, 174, 200
winter rules, 200
Wolf game, 187
woods. *See also* drivers
    defined, 200
    fairway, 6, 39, 55
    head covers for, 5

Y

yardage marker, 200
yellow stakes, 172, 200
yips, 200

Perfectly
portable!

With handy, compact *VISUAL*™ *Quick Tips* books, you're in the know wherever you go.

All *VISUAL*™ *Quick Tips* books pack a lot of info into a compact 5 x 7 $1/8$″ guide you can toss into your tote bag or brief case for ready reference.

Look for these and other *VISUAL*™ *Quick Tips* books wherever books are sold.

Read Less-Learn More®

Visual®
An Imprint of ⊕**WILEY**